# Oh Crap!  Now What?
## *The Home Edition*

# 6 easy steps to master life long stress relief and perfect health

Written by Ani Wilson

**Copyright**

First Printing: July 2014

ISBN 978-0473-29239-3

Ani Wilson, Auckland 0630, New Zealand

www.Thehealthhug.com

# The Passive Book

## Introduction

You've picked up this book, probably by accident, out of casual interest in the cover or the crazy title. Or you know, somewhere deep inside that there is something 'not quite right' about your life or your health.

All of your life you've been told to make decisions based on what your head tells you, and not to pay attention to your heart. Or at least that's my story. But sometimes when you get that little feeling in the pit of your stomach, or in the recess of your heart, you just know something to be true.

I hope this book activates within you that same inner feeling. Whatever the reason is that brings you to open its pages today, it grows into a stronger question, and is complimented by a resounding "aha!" moment for you as you read on.

**So here goes!**

From the age of 18 through to 28 (10 years) I wasn't sick once. I was extremely happy in my life; I travelled the world, fell in love twice, and was paid to do what I loved to do. And then I settled down.

Settling was a fearful word for me. I didn't WANT to settle, but the man of my dreams was 7 years older, had been married before and was ready to start a family. My options were to settle down, or leave the partnership. Obviously, for the purposes of this story, I stayed, and I settled. Or at least I tried.

---

Where my heart was adventurous and wanted to travel, his heart wanted to take seed. He started to build a house, and we moved further away from friends and family. My holidays away were no longer spent in a tent by the side of the road; they were spent in 5 star hotels with room service. I struggled. I didn't know it then, but everything about the relationship went against my inner need for adventure and social interaction. My family and friends were all congratulating me on my "catch" and on the outside I felt nothing could be more wonderful. However, my soul was dying and being replaced by someone else's projection of me.

I tried to get pregnant for years, but knew whole-heartedly that I wouldn't conceive if my mind wasn't ready. For three years I suffered with psoriasis, and had been told by dermatologists and doctors alike, that there was no known cure or cause. They *assumed* the cause was from stress, but I couldn't understand what stress I was facing. To me, at the time, I was happy. I loved my job. I loved my partner. What more could I want? Why would psoriasis be so prevalent in my life if I was so happy?

After 6 years, we got married. And I started to cough. I woke every night at 2am and coughed on average for 40 minutes. I tried everything - I had tests done. I even coughed up blood on the nights when my coughing became too intense. I thought perhaps I had an allergy, but I had the all clear from the many doctors I saw. I was told I probably had the left over remnants from an old chest infection, but there was no evidence to support that claim. I was also told that there was a 90 day cough going around. Hang on, lets count the days... 90 days does not make 5 months...no?

To the medical specialists, I was the bill of health and was sent home to ponder my growing ailments.

So here's the thing: The moment I told my husband that I wanted to leave him, I slept soundly (in a different room obviously!) and was never affected by that cough again.

The day I left the house and began my new life, my psoriasis vanished, which in itself is a miracle considering the scale of skin flakes peeling off my scalp at the time! Remember, psoriasis has no medical cure. I knew something was changing inside me when I noticed the difference in my health. Immediately I started to ponder, is my health within my control?

Years later when I was diagnosed with Grade 3 Breast Cancer I was not at all shocked. I knew I had allowed the Cancer to form, and I knew why it had appeared. I was a chronic sufferer of stress for many years due to my work ethic and type A tendencies for order and achievement, so I accepted that my immunity would be lowered and that something might eventuate.

But what I didn't realise at the time, and what I wasn't prepared for, was the volume of people who I'd known for years who began telling me their own life troubles, that they too had suffered in silence from an illness or indeed Cancer. And as I sat in the Chemo ward every Thursday allowing a form of mustard gas to be injected into my then healthy body, I began to pay attention to the people around me, telling me of their stress, their overwhelm, and of their emotional struggles. I saw only pain; I felt only despair emanating from those around me. It bugged me. Their cries to turn back time started to chip away silently at my core.

The common message from each and every gorgeous lady in that ward was that they should have done precisely what the Oncologist ordered - to slow down. The very same Oncologist, bless him, had told me exactly those instructions on numerous occasions. Each time they were delivered I smiled sweetly and said something smart and funny to dispel the truth behind those words. "Another day, perhaps" would be my regular thought behind any such spoken word.

In fact, when other people I knew were taking days off work after their chemo sessions to recuperate, I would bring not only my laptop, but also my cellphone and iPad to the hospital and work, work, work, planning meetings only an hour after my injections were complete, giving me *just* enough time to speed my way back to the office.

The only feeling I had, was that of embarrassment from the horrific bulge under my work clothes where a port-a-cath had been 'installed' in my chest.

I was more worried about how I was seen, rather than how I actually felt. I was (and to be fair, still am) a proud woman, who didn't feel any need to worry others about what I was emotionally or physically going through. I certainly did not want to bother anyone with my 'boring' or 'self-pitying' story. And thus the only reason I eventually told my boss at the time that I had the Cancer, was to prepare him for the eventual loss of my hair.

What came next was a defining chapter in my journey, and something I certainly was not expecting.

After giving 120% effort at all times to the corporate giant where I worked, I was asked formally by the leadership team of that company to wear a realistic wig at all times so as not to impact the confidence of my then clients. It struck me then; my leadership team had forgotten what it was like to be human. They were focused on profits and never once sent me a 'get well soon' card, or any message of support.

To add the final nail in my coffin, I opted to take only 2 necessary days off work to recover from life saving breast cancer surgery, as I was so worried about the state of my account, and the real possibility of being replaced at the head of that account.

My work place and my leadership team had taken the humanity out of *me* also.

4 weeks after my surgery, my wonderful manager told me he had paid for me to attend a once yearly conference. What this meant, was that I would be offline

from my clients and resources for an entire business day. I couldn't fathom it and so I kindly declined the offer.

"Too late" he said. "You're booked"

Although I reluctantly attended that day, it was the day that changed my life forever. It was the day that someone finally got through my harsh exterior and hit me, *bam*, in the heart.

I was sitting in the front row of the auditorium for an after lunch key note speech, when tears started streaming down my face. I looked around; no one else seemed to be crying. I looked back at the man on the stage; he seemed only to be speaking to me. His message was profound, in that he was storytelling about how his life had changed when one morning he woke up ad found he couldn't move. He had severe burn out and it took him an entire week to get up out of that bed.

As he told us about his symptoms, I knew and checked off each and every one of them. As he told us about the impact his work life had on his personal life, I too could relate. But when he looked at me and said "Life is too important to be giving all your energy to someone who doesn't give a damn" I completely lost all dignity and control.

I had fallen victim to the corporate world of stress. I gave more of my energy each day, to my employers than I did to my own family and partner.

I resented being a mum because it drained my energy stores further, and I gave nothing back when my partner wanted social interaction. I had become an emotional retard.

Two months after my Cancer diagnosis, the laser-beam signal attached to my senses to pick up on other stressed women was highly attuned. The intensity of the problem was becoming all too obvious. Now that I knew the level of the epidemic, and how hard these women (as had I) were trying to shake off the social burdens of being sick whilst trying to be a good mother, partner, housecleaner and worker, I just had to take action, and I had to save myself first in order to then save the people around me.

And so I set out on a mission. This is my story of discovery and empowerment.

# *Prologue*

It seems that these days we have at all times, information telling us how to drive, how to behave, what to do and what not to do, what to eat and what not to eat.

We live in a world where information is so accessible to us via a laptop, that you can be anywhere in the world and still have access to the same information that someone has from the other side of the planet. The iPhone is the 2nd highest selling item in history (1st being the Rubik's Cube!), with over 89% of the developing world having a mobile phone when most can't afford to even open a bank account! With so much information readily available at our fingertips things can seem a bit overwhelming!

Do a Google search on the term "Terminal illness" and you'll receive over 9.8 million hits, Google "Stress relief" and you'll receive over 53 Million results! "Inner Health", 140 Million hits! "Life Balance", 427 Million results!

No wonder we're on information overload!

When I started on this mission, I was trying to find the Holy Grail of stress relief – the one source of all truth that could fix me instantly without the need to learn meditation, spend lots of money or quit my job. Instead, life threw me a curve ball and made me work hard for this outcome! Really hard! I didn't slow down; in fact I proceeded to spend the next 4 years on full speed ahead. With the intensity of this passion, I was hoping to evade this same consequence for you, the reader.

I spent those years searching the Internet, reading hundreds of books, certifying in new practices, attending every webinar and seminar I could, watching tutorials on

You Tube daily, and performing trials using myself as a Guinea Pig. I accumulated information from around the world in order to classify and determine only the most relevant information to ensure there was a ONE STOP repository for you to access on your journey towards being the best YOU that you can be!

And I believe, wholeheartedly, that I've finally done it.

Can I relax now? No way! I strive to learn something new every day, and I have come to realise that part of my own stress management journey was to fulfill the need to expand my mind. However, these days I do it with excitement and with a smile on my face instead of constant worry lines on my brow. I finally found what worked for me after years of trying literally hundreds of stress management techniques and I've witnessed how my own story and findings have had a profound impact on my clients and friends. Do I still attract a level of stress? Hell Yes. I cannot control the actions of others. However, I fully accept the outcome of how their actions impact me, as I know that is within my control.

After practicing life coaching for a number of years using all the tried and true psychological processes successfully on clients I suddenly had an epiphany. A friend came to me one evening and asked what had helped me in my *own* journey to stress relief. And I struggled to answer her due to my fear of being judged. What if she thought I was strange? What if, as I told her my own story her eyes showed signs of boredom or bewilderment?

I started out trying to tell her of the 'well known' life coaching techniques, but she kept asking the same question over and over: "Is that what YOU did?"

And so with resignation I said something that I had been avoiding telling my clients for years, "No. To be honest, I used a completely different set of techniques on my own journey!"

Bam! Doesn't that mean I was a fraud?

I thank God that I surround myself with such insightful friends who don't judge me, or expect too much from me. My friend simply looked at me kindly and smiled. I knew at that moment that I had stumbled on to the truth.

Why did I feel I couldn't share those techniques with others if I believed so deeply in their success?

What was I afraid of revealing about myself whilst secretly harbouring all this knowledge within?

So I went offline for a few months, and I dug deep, and I wrote and I wrote and I wrote. I wrote about all the techniques I had used, and really ruminated on which of those techniques really had made the biggest difference. And from that exercise I developed a Do It Yourself challenge for beating stress – the WOF Challenge that cuts through the red tape and allows you to take control back of your SELF within only a few weeks. It's a starting point – but one that is powerful, costs no money at all and can not be reversed if you dedicate to it whole heartedly, as I do each day.

During my journey I found something else very interesting was happening to me. As I opened my eyes to the effortless ease of relieving my own stress, I began to notice through performing those same steps that I could heal other physical ailments without any need for medical intervention.

This discovery was enlightening, remarkable and a life changer for me. I now choose never to be sick again as

I know it's an outcome that is fully within my own control. When I hear others talk about how they always get a cold 'this time of the year' I smile and don't enter in to any returned discussion. Like politics, what you choose to believe is exactly that; YOUR belief, not mine.

My purpose within this book is to cut through the crap, get right to the heart of the message, and stop wasting time with fads and passing theories. I've done the work for you.

The DIY Challenges I have developed don't follow your usual path of 'mind, body, and spirit'. I found many of the life coach stress management techniques, although wonderful and hugely successful for others, took me into deeper regret and opened further the cracks that were forming elsewhere in my life. As I noticed a frustration in my work life, I then saw I was unhappy in my relationship. As I delved into my relationship, I found I was harbouring dissatisfaction with my house. As I investigated what it was about my living space that caused me despair I ventured into blaming others for my shortfall in available time. As I complained about being time poor, I focused on its impact on my health. And the cycle of reviewing my life and its HUGELY disappointing factors just seemed to get bigger and bigger until I realised that I was, after all of the soul searching, MORE overwhelmed by it all than I was when I began!

In addition to that, the more articles I read, the more information that started piling in to my inbox. In my quest to ask the right questions, I attracted thousands of 'helpful' responses from those who had firm beliefs one way or another. In my effort to reduce my own stress, I became somewhat more fatigued.

But over time and rippling away in the background, I realized I was doing the right things, listening to my mind and body, and building an amazing resilience to it all. With all the information that was flooding in, I started to see that information is not knowledge.

Information does not ensure knowingness.

My work life started to change. I started using my intuition above all else when making hard decisions, and my energy came back in droves.

What was it I found? What was the secret to having it all? What is the secret to moving from Anger to Forgiveness in only a few short moments?

What is the secret to moving from tiredness to energized instantly?

There is only one true answer and I now happily take this secret in to every boardroom I enter. My knowingness allowed me to define a shortcut to loving life again. This shortcut is explained in this book.

My techniques are simple, they're direct and any 'no-bullshit, crazed "I don't have time" work-aholic' can follow these easy steps. By the way, that description was me only a few years ago, so I can relate! If you asked my boss or any of my colleagues what I was like? Their answer would have been "very similar to the energizer bunny, only with skates on!"

You may have seen many versions of the "Life Wheel" that include the word "balance" in many forms - to me, I found that total health was the starting point to finding the PERFECT ME. But what is total health? I believe it can be depicted in this very basic diagram. Start here, and the rest will follow.

Physical
Health =
Nutrition +
Body

Ego =
Knowledge +
Beliefs +
Intuition

Attitude +
Emotion

The
Perfect
ME

Experience +
Social Fun

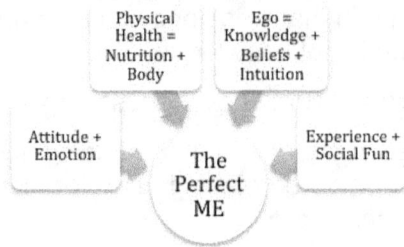

So if you've ever had the following thoughts come into your mind, then this book is definitely for you!

- Why am I the only one in the family that seems to get sick all the time?
- I don't have time to try these 'new age' rubbish techniques! Give me something I can really sink my teeth into!
- I am so tired!! I feel like I need a few weeks off just to sleep and catch up, but I have a household to run and support and no one else will help!
- I hate the fact that I'm increasingly snappy at my kids!
- I am so sick of these aches and pains! I'm taking so many drugs, I feel like a chemist!
- Hurry up and get on with it!

Welcome to the beginning of your path to enlightened health.

# *How to use this book*

Obviously any author is going to tell you to read the whole darn book! "Get your moneys worth!" But although every page does offer tips and tidbits of information, you are free to jump sections and go straight to chapters that are of most relevance at the time of reading.

This book has been compiled in three parts; the Passive Book is filled with research and analogies to help with your understanding of your body's mechanics, and I've used myself as a guinea pig to help to show fact from fiction through its pages.

The DIY Bible is where you'll find the shortest path to health and stress relief once and for all.

And the Active Book is where I tell you how to easily heal yourself from 'every day' aches and pains. Keep this book handy, as it is meant to become a type of encyclopedia, to be there as your best friend through different stages of your life.

If you DO jump sections, I guide you to take stock of your whole life, not just the current affliction, and be honest with yourself. Perhaps it is time for a full and total clean up?

And of course, if you **don't** want to be healthy, happy, and live a wonderful life, I warn you; don't read on!

# Chapter One - The Essential Overview

Too many of us these days are caught in a flurry of activity, surrounded by noise, confronted with a million choices to make in one day, manic beyond belief with an endless to-do list, and are plagued by the Grandparents synopsis of how *they* managed when they were our age.

In no other time in the history of human population of Earth have we been so accessible to so many people at all hours of every day. You catch up on phone calls when you're stuck in traffic waiting to drop your child off at school; you sneak a peak at your inbox when the traffic light goes red and quickly respond to 3 or 4 'urgent' emails. Your phone beeps when you've snuck to the toilet, meaning invariably you rush your deed to make sure it wasn't an important call you've missed. Your boss has you on speed dial and won't hesitate to contact you late into the evening.

Gone are the days where, if you were not at home, you were unreachable. 'Back then', there were no background sounds to distract you. You could commit to your family 100% instead of checking Facebook whilst multitasking by pushing your child on the swing. And, other than by your in-laws, you weren't being told what to do, how to do it, and when to do it!

Today your inbox accumulates more information in one day than a man living in the early 1900's would assimilate in a year! The amount of information and input into our minds is growing daily. Technology is speeding full tilt ahead to allow this to happen. In 2014 they discovered a new path for data transfer that's faster than our current means, using diamonds.  Who's to say they won't discover an even faster method in 2018?  How are we meant to keep up?  Have our brains become faster at processing this information too?  I think not.

How sad is it that there is now an iPhone App that beeps at you every hour to remind you to take a break and breathe for 10 seconds!  When did we leave our senses behind and become such a crazed bunch of techno-heads?  And with it, our count of depression, anxiety and stress has sky rocketed.  Across the globe 1 in 4 women are prescribed some form of anti-depressant medication; a figure that is startling but when you look around and truly witness within your own city, you can understand why.  We're all in such a rush.

And don't think for a moment that the person at your workplace who seems to 'have it all together" isn't also struggling internally with time constraints and moments of chaos.  But what is it that makes some of us cave and some seem to sail through with no care in the world?

Why is it that some people always seem to get the latest bug that's floating around the office, and others are never afflicted?

Why do some people suffer from back pain regularly, or easily get sprains from simply walking to the shops, when others run across continents without getting any injury at all?

Why do some people suffer through medical interventions and others tell you that they found the whole process a breeze?

And why, when told they have only months to live do some people bounce back and live a full harmonious life when others become frail and die as predicted by their doctor?

What is it that makes these people different? What is the explanation or equation?

The answer is simple but many of us choose to ignore it, thinking its some New Age mumbo Jumbo. However, there are thousands of new scientific studies that tell us now what our Ancestors knew thousands of years ago. We need to get back to the basics and stop living like robots.

Again, the answer is truly simple and it can be contained in just one word

FOCUS

You've heard the adage "Where focus goes, energy flows"? Well it's true and more meaningful than you realise. Don't stop reading just yet. Believe me; I was raised in a corporate climate, have Type A tendencies, am an over achiever and don't have a 'hippie' cell in my body. But I can attest that by following even 80% of what is in this book, your world will change. Focus on what matters and your world will turn upside down.

Your health will improve dramatically. Your relationships will improve. Your energy will increase. **Your stress levels will reduce.** Your patience with your children will be at an all time high. **And you will begin to enjoy life, and see it for what it truly is;**

**…A big fat adventure.**

When I started out on this journey, I was overwhelmed at the amount of conflicting information that could be found on the Internet and also within the Medical industry. There seemed to be so many new websites dedicated to debunking statements made by medical influencers and new research appearing daily that opened holes in beliefs we'd formed over many decades.

What I eventually found was that once you focused on the simplicity of the human body and brain, the answer to the future of stress relief and healing was glaringly obvious. **We have simply chosen to forget how to help ourselves, and willingly choose to allow *others* to fix or heal us.**

During my seminars if I ask for my audience to raise their hands if they know how to relieve stress, 90% of attendees keep their hands lowered, thinking quietly "what a silly question, why would I be here if I knew?!" But surely we all know the answer?  Surely stress hasn't been impacting your life to this effect since the early days of childhood?  Surely there have been times in your life when you instinctively knew how to work hard and then relax and unwind efficiently when you got home?

Think back to your early 20's and you'll recall a sense of freedom and expectation for the wondrous things to come.

I challenge that you have simply forgotten how easy it is, and now choose to believe that life is hard.  The more you focus on how stressed you are, the more stress that seemingly comes in to your life.   Am I right?

Have you ever noticed that when something goes terribly wrong, other bad things come your way? (Watch out, you know what they say!  Bad things always come in 3s!)  When you feel stressed, other stressful moments compound and can leave you feeling attacked.

The way to stop stress in its tracks is to focus your thoughts elsewhere, to retrain your brain to reclaim your youthful awareness and lust for life.

Your thoughts are powerful and you have full command over where they travel. By neglecting your basic need to see wonder in this world, you have allowed stress and injury to occur.

When you feel an ache or pain within your body, it is the MIND that has caused this ache to occur.

I know this is a bold statement to make, hence the bold type, but it truly is that simple! Once you know this for a fact, your health will take a positive turn almost immediately.

It's OK; I don't expect you to believe me just yet. And I know you're yelling at the book right now "Focus my thoughts elsewhere?!! I WOULD IF I COULD!!" grumble, grumble, grumble…. Yes?

Once I realized that the human presence was made up of three elements; the brain, the body and the mind that controls everything I had the power of choice to take back control of my mind which allowed me the grace to use myself as a guinea pig and test this healing theory.

**I cured myself of arthritic fingers within 3 days**, removed the need for expensive reading glasses almost overnight and resolved a 3 year ailment of psoriasis without the need of any kind of outside intervention.

I'm a believer; so let's see if we can't do the same for you.

# Chapter Two  -Understanding your makeup

Since the inception of the doctrine of Materialism at the beginning of the 19ₜₕ century, (in western society anyway) we started asking ourselves "Why is my body doing this to me!?" instead of asking the age old question "Why am I doing this to my body?"  Eastern cultures still understand this and still practice the art of reflexology and meditation for inner healing, but we westerner's seem to need a written note from our doctor to stop and pay attention.

If you stop asking yourself "What am I dying of?" and start asking, "What am I living for?" your world will begin to change immediately.

My message is clear; stop dealing with your dis-ease or discontent and start dealing with your Self.

If you take the time to research into each case where spontaneous remission occurred to terminally ill patients, you will find that every one of those people made a firm decision to let go of their ego (their firm beliefs and outer self) and decided to live life to the full with new passion and wonder.

Ask yourself, if you knew you had only 2 weeks to live, how would you spend it?  Would you worry about your bills, what your friends thought of your outfit, what your mother may have said to you yesterday?

I would counter, not.  You wouldn't waste this time thinking about the past, or things you could not control, or spend it complaining about the weather.  You'd call your friends to have a laugh rather than a grumble.

You'd make time to go outside to enjoy the warmth of the sun, and you'd stop and smell those darn roses!

You would grab any fear you had and take the leap anyway.

Have you ever stressed about an up coming presentation you had to arrange at work? You were stressed because you thought you couldn't control the outcome or what people thought of you. But what if you had looked at the same presentation and walked in there not caring one ounce about what anyone thought, and just set your mindset on enjoying the moment of being in the limelight! What a different outcome and experience you would have had.

And in those last days you would seek out fun. Actually scrap that; you would seek out, *and find* **Fun** (with a bold capital F!)

I never get over the amount of people I meet who are just surviving in their daily lives - people who have spent years creating a mask that hides their inner torment and struggle. With a simple word, their world can crumble, and tears start forming in their eyes. We each have a need to be happy yet we fight against that need daily until one day we explode through exhaustion.


As human beings we are gifted an average of 30,000 days here on earth. That's not really that much. Some of us choose to enjoy this time, yet most of us spend 20,000 of those days complaining, focusing on regret, looking backward, being fearful and suffering from pain or illness. Why are we doing this to ourselves?

In less than 1 year, you recycle 98% of all molecular matter in your body. You regenerate your stomach lining every 5 days, your liver every 6 weeks, and a new skin once a month. As cells leave your body, they pass on their cellular memory to the newly generated cells; hence unless you change the memory patterns of those cells, a 'nasty' cell sitting in the midst of them all can remain untouched for years and grow into a tumor that is then deemed 'normal' by your 'killer' lymphocytes.

Your mind has the power to change this memory pattern and to enhance your immunity once more. It is your choice; Grow, or Grow a Tumor.

You MUST know that your body is THE most amazing system in the Universe! As I can't reach through this book to shake your shoulders and start yelling at you to pay attention, know these truly interesting, awe inspiring facts about

YOU

- Your visual cortex can distinguish over 14 Million shades of colour

- The focusing muscles in your eye move around 100,000x a day, which is equivalent to your legs taking you for an 80km walk daily for the rest of your life! (Phew!)

- 1-7 Billion Liver cells are regenerated every second!

- Your nose can recall over 50,000 different scents

- There are over 100,000 miles of blood vessels in the average human body

- In your lifetime, you will produce enough saliva to fill 2 average sized swimming pools

- There are 70 Kilometres of nerves in your skin

- If uncoiled, the DNA in all your cells in your body would stretch 10 Billion miles – that's the equivalent distance from earth to Pluto and back

- The human neck has the same amount of bones as a Giraffe

Amazed? You should be. You are not just a pile of bones and muscles sent to live this life to watch it fly by from the comfort of your couch. Your life has been gifted to you. What you do with it is your choice. However, if you're slowing down either with age or due to the amount of burden you're carrying, then I suggest changing how and what you do NOW. We all know someone who has moved into a nursing home and seemingly lost the will to live and someone else who has chosen to "thrive". Why?

Your brain is made up of over 100 Billion neurons, each with over 10,000 simultaneous synaptic connections to other neurons. To show the power of this, imagine you're standing in a sports stadium filled with over 10,000 other screaming fans, and being able to consciously, and coherently communicate simultaneously with every other person there. This is exactly what your brain is doing every second of every day. **There is no other such complex system yet discovered in the entire Universe.**

...In the ENTIRE UNIVERSE!!

Why are we so amazing, yet so misguided and lost?

The mind is our mission control. It activates the brain, which regulates the flow of energy and information through your whole body. The electricity generated in your brain when you are awake is sufficient to activate a light bulb at any time. Your brain is your healing factory - you just need to turn on the power.

Know this; there is no physical experience without a corresponding neural experience.

If you feel pain, your Thalamus has been activated to tell you of the pain.

If you have an emotional experience, your Limbic brain fires up

If you feel Fear, you activate your Amygdala.

When you judge something or someone, you spark neural activity in your Frontal Lobe

When you walk or wave, you activate the motor cortex of your Parietal lobe

If you're overheating or too cold, your Hypothalamus tells your body to sweat or shiver

When you close your eyes and imagine a scene, you use the same part of your brain as you would if your eyes were open and actually seeing that scene; that being the occipital lobe.

Our mind is the dominant factor in all that we do. It rules our perception, and can often manipulate our reality by playing chaos with our brain function.

No truer reflection of this statement is when you hear of patients who have suffered an amputation, who claim to feel pain in the limb that has been removed. This common complaint is known within the medical journals as "Psychogenic Pain" – pain perception with no obvious physical cause.  The patient's brain has a memory of pain, and *believes* the pain to be true.  And thus it is felt.

Your thoughts, feelings and emotions are all translated into NEURAL activity.  Mind and Body (which includes the brain) is ONE process.  The thoughts you generate trigger neural activity to specific areas of your body.  When you focus on stress or worry or negativity or fear, your body's natural flow of energy is interrupted or dulled.

When you are stressed don't you often also feel unwell, break out in a rash, or show symptoms of diarrhea or constipation?   So when a child shows these same symptoms without any obvious virus plaguing their school, why do we not stop and ask the child what they are feeling?  9 times out of 10, their rash or vomiting or toilet spills are a direct symptom from an emotional issue that they are holding within.

Once you understand the power of your thoughts, your perception, and your beliefs as they relate to the neural activity in your brain, then you will come to realise that ALL external influencers or stressors play a role in your inner body health and external reflection of that health.

You could eat what you believe is the healthiest diet ever and still put on weight or become unwell if your thoughts are focused on negative outcomes.  "I expect to get a cold about 3x a year" and thus you will.

If you drove to work every day and the traffic was always chaotic and stressful, odds are that one day you would crash.  The same analogy is used for our daily lives; chaos + stress = crash.

What would you do if people around you were driving erratically?  You'd slow down, you'd be cautious, and you'd avoid high traffic areas.  Imagine driving that way for years, being cautious, being scared, and then finding yourself in a high-speed zone in rush hour yet again.  You wouldn't know what to do, as you might've forgotten how to deal with that simple situation.  You'd be so stressed; you'd probably pull over and wait until all the other cars had gone, and your heart rate had returned to normal.  This, my friend, is what we call "Burnout".

The problem with chronic, ongoing stress is that we don't function at optimal speed, we over react to things, and we manifest all sorts of physical and mental ailments.

Change your thoughts, and you'll change your actions and inevitably the outcome.

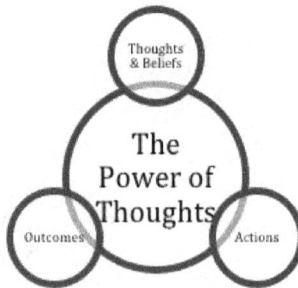

I love a quote from the "Course of Miracles" that states that when you sacrifice yourself to other people, you make them the thief. Effectively they are stealing your energy, your time, your emotional kindness, taking up your thoughts, and benefiting from your interaction in a one way exchange.

The more hats you wear, the more time you extend for other people's purposes, the more things you try to achieve in one day – the less of yourself you will have left over.

Think of yourself as a pie. Cut it 8 ways, and by the end of the day, you're left with crumbs with which to survive. One day you'll wake up with the feeling that you've lost your identity or sense of "self" somewhere along the way and many of us then choose to resent life and the world for taking it away.

To recover from those ailments and outcomes, you need to take back control of your body by **empowering your MIND**.

Simple.

---

*"1000 candles can be lit from a single candle, and the life of that candle will not be shortened" - Buddha*

40

# Chapter Three – Genetics

I was told when I was emotionally low after the birth of my second child; by my mother that she had suffered from postnatal depression after she had me, and that in the early 70's this was considered a possible genetic tendency. When medical professionals tell us something invariably we are at a loss to challenge this statement, as we don't have sufficient information to counter what we are being told. And thus a thought festers and sits for years and forms into a firm belief that can impact our decisions later in life.

I look back and wonder how many false statements were made to me over the years, whether by teachers, mentors, friends or professionals, and how many have lodged themselves into my mind as firm beliefs.

We now know that even if there is a genetic disposition within a family toward a particular physical ailment, such as heart disease, that we have the power to manipulate the constitution of our DNA and remove this genetic probability.

Thanks to luminaries such as Dr Masaru Emoto and Dr. Bruce Lipton, we now have groundbreaking evidence to conclusively show us that through changing our environment and manipulating our thoughts, WE alone can change the physical structure of a single DNA strand. We can heal our own DNA should we fully believe and want to make it happen.

Research supports the statement that genetics are attributable to 4% of all illness, but we now have the power to reduce this percentage.

If 86% of all illness and disease is caused by emotional stress, 4% by genetics and 10 % our environment, through the power of thought alone, you can reduce your probability of attracting sickness in to your life by 90%.

Isn't that cause for a celebration of life?

# Chapter Four – Stress, the Almighty

In 1954 the amount of the world population impacted by Cancer was 17%. This statistic alone is staggering. It is astounding that so many of the 2 Billion people (at that time) on this earth could be impacted by such a grave disease.

By 2012, this statistic had increased exponentially to over 76%. Knowing that the world population is now almost 8 Billion, over ¾ of the people on this planet will come into contact with Cancer at some time in their lives. The Cancer Research industry is now worth over $3Billion a year; yay for them - not such great news for us.

We allow ourselves to be injected with a form of mustard gas that is outlawed by the Geneva Convention and call this medical intervention Chemotherapy. And although the chemicals being used by oncologists these days are more targeted to specific cells or organs in our body, we are still allowing the medical arena to kill off whole portions of our body without ever asking why.

Did you know that Oncologists are told to no longer offer the percentage chance of your recovery when they give you a diagnosis of Cancer? The power of our own minds over the healing process is so well known, over 52% of all doctors in the United States admitted to using placebos when prescribing patients with drugs in a recent survey in 2012. Cancer survival rates are mirroring the mental expectation of the patients if caught pre-terminal. If told by their doctor that they would be dead within a few months, the clients' mental state was instantly almost shocked in to submission in to letting that scenario eventuate. It is your choice whether you believe the statistical evidence from your doctor when he tells you of your chance of survival or recovery. But when you realize there is no such thing as statistics when every single person on this earth has a completely different genetic model and background you must wonder why we so willingly believe them.

If you visited the doctor at the turn of last century, they would have spent an hour with you asking about life, your family and your worries in order to determine the cause of your ailment. Today however, you spend hours in a waiting room, only to catch a 15-minute glimpse of your doctor, who focuses on the specific ailment at hand and prescribes you a synthetically produced drug to help.

When our bodies are nature's most amazing chemists, why do we spend so much money on over the counter prescriptions?

And when did life suddenly become such a rush?

You can leave your doctors surgery with a pill for your irritable bowel, another pill for your sleeplessness, yet another pill for your back pain, and more pills for your anxiety or depression!

You may know someone who takes 3 pills a day as prescribed by their physician and still ingests a myriad of multi vitamins and health tablets because of the impact of some sales pitch on TV. To me, that sounds like an expensive habit to maintain.


We look to our nutrition to offer us further insights and resolutions. However there are so many different types of diets on the market today, who should we believe? Which one should we try?

We are each born with all the nutrient forming systems in our bodies that we could possibly need. The only vitamin that the human body does not naturally produce is Vitamin C. Instead of popping a bunch of pills on a daily basis, should we not be asking ourselves why our body is not naturally regulating the production of those hormones or vitamins?

When we are diagnosed with an illness or a disease, why does your doctor immediately prescribe a course of action to remove the disease, and not open discussion about what it was that potentially CAUSED the disease in the first place?

Because he doesn't have TIME.

When I meet with a client regarding stress I always ask whether they also have any physical pain or recurring illness. After regaling to me their understanding of their emotional stress, most clients tell me they are quite healthy and look at me as if I'm taking quite a sideways tangent to their consult time.

Once they relax and learn to trust in me however, they begin to mention their back pain, or finger pain, neck tightness, heart palpitations, skin rash, asthma, bowel problems, and the list goes on. It seems that most people forget to mention their health concern, as they have become accustomed to it in their lives!

Stop fooling yourself. Why tell someone you are healthy and fine, when if you paid attention to what your body is trying to tell you, you would see there is a pattern in your ailments?

If it is now well accepted that over 86% of all illness and disease is attributable to emotional stress (this statistic is realistically more to the tune of 90-95%) how DOES emotional stress impact our body and take control over our lives?

Stress is not an emotion. It is something that happens TO us, rather than how we feel. The word "stressed" simply means that we are not coping with the amount of stressors in our lives, or the perception of those stressors.

Let me be clear; **Stress is not our natural state**. It is a learned state that MUST be unlearned.

Stressors can come in any form. It may be someone, something, our environment, a situation or even a type of food as depicted in the diagram below.

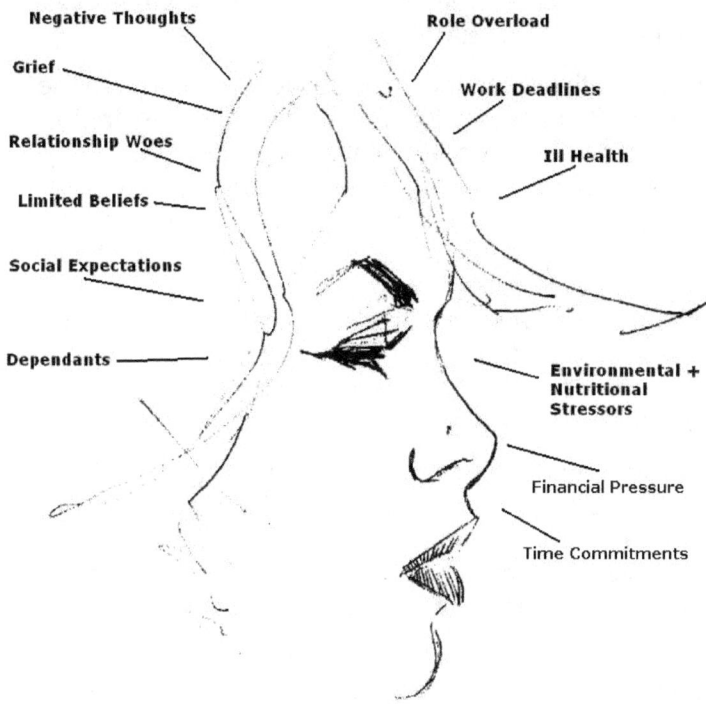

Negative Thoughts
Grief
Relationship Woes
Limited Beliefs
Social Expectations
Dependants
Role Overload
Work Deadlines
Ill Health
Environmental + Nutritional Stressors
Financial Pressure
Time Commitments

Here's a scenario you may recognize:

Have you ever gone for a walk after dinner in your local neighbourhood, a walk you've probably done hundreds of times, when one evening, lost in thought, you realise the sun has gone and darkness has descended. You look up to find there is no one else around. When only 5 mins before you were happy and enjoying your walk, you are now feeling anxious to get home! Your breathing quickens, your energy seems to come out of nowhere allowing you to speed home in record time, and your thoughts are filled with scenes out of some scary movie.  Can you relate?

Take another scenario.  You've woken up and realised you are 30 mins late for work already.  You instantly jump out of bed and are on full alert to ensure all of your usual morning tasks are done at speed.  You're now ready to go but can't find the keys.  You buzz around the house, bumping into things whilst cursing.  You finally find the keys and run out the door frantically only to find that you're now stuck in horrendous traffic.  Instantly you feel frustration towards all the other people also stuck in their cars, and think "Why me!?  Why now!?"  Sound familiar?

In both scenarios your heart rate instantly spiked, your blood pressure went up, your blood platelets got sticky, blood rushed from your extremities to your organs and your breathing rate increased.  You effectively became Wonder Woman / Superman in the blink of an eye.

The only down side to that was your ability to remain calm and think clearly was effectively washed away with the redirection of blood flow away from the brain which is why often you won't see something that is directly in front of your eyes (your keys) and can quickly begin to place judgment and blame on factors outside your control (the other drivers).   Your perception influenced your experience.


Imagine if you will, if you had bounded out of bed with a smile on your face, had a long hot shower, and called your boss to tell him you'd be an hour late.  How different would your day have been?

To drive this point home further, imagine if you will that you're a bride getting married to a wonderful farmer whose family had toiled his land for generations. For 4 years his farm had suffered through drought. On the day of the wedding, of course it rains. To you, it has ruined your day. To your new husband, it was a gift from God. Your perception influenced your experience.

Change your perception and you'll master your experience.

Once you begin to effectively eradicate stress from your life, your radar for stressed out people will then be on high alert. Just as when you buy a new car you suddenly see that car everywhere. For now though you may seem to be lost in that forest of trees and can't see the wood. In today's world, we are more on edge, highly strung and stressed than ever before.

Expectations from our employers, our children, our family, or partners are higher, and we've succumbed to being more than we can cope with in order to survive and compete.

Most people admit to wearing multiple hats. Gone are the days when you had one role and you did it well.

I will imply it again: The prevalence of Cancer has seen a dramatic increase by over 347% in the past 5 decades. New infectious diseases are being found and named every year all thanks to that looming cloud we call Stress.

You can't stop a disease from showing up in your town, but you can darn well stop it from impacting YOU. If everyone in the world were to stop relying on pills and miracle cures, but instead build up their own resiliency to disease by balancing their internal systems and thoughts, the world would effectively eradicate itself from illness overnight.

---

*"Every day one should at least hear one little song, read one good poem, see one fine painting and -- if at all possible -- speak a few sensible words."*
*— Johann Wolfgang von Goethe*

---

So what is this thing we call stress exactly?

The original meaning for the word stress has its origins from the Construction industry. Stress was described as the total load a bridge or entity could withstand before it was considered unsound.

Hungarian researcher Dr. Hans Selye borrowed the term for his pioneering work into the condition during the 1930's. He described STRESS as the bodies "non-specific response to any demand, pleasant or not".

Again, stress is NOT an emotion. It is a term used to describe our tolerance to internal and external situations.

Two people can have entirely different reactions to the same stressor; one may be stressed by the situation, and the other could take it in their stride and think nothing of it. The difference in reaction is due to their opposing perceptions.

The list below is a compilation of symptoms formed after long exposure to stress, also commonly known as chronic stress. Of course if you watch a scary movie and someone jumps out from behind the curtain, your body does some instant crazy and amazing things, but you'll thankfully be able to calm down once the movie has ended, knowing you just witnessed an attack of acute stress.

Chronic stress however creeps up on you slowly. To begin, you may only suffer from a few of these symptoms, however if left unchecked, more and more boxes are ticked and we spiral into deeper problems such as anxiety and depression.

You may well know the psychological symptoms and skim through these, but I tempt you to slow your gaze when reading through the physical symptoms. Many of these common ailments go unnoticed as an outcome of our stressful lives. Watch out for these, and reflect on how you are feeling emotionally when these symptoms occur.

**Psychological Symptoms of Stress**:

- Forgetfulness
- Emotional
- Feeling Overwhelmed
- Tearful
- Unnerved or nervous
- Lowered self esteem
- Indecisive
- Depression
- Lowered creativity
- Increased doubt
- Mood imbalances
- Prone to seeing the negative
- Loss of ability to find humour
- Quicker to anger
- Clumsiness

My first onslaught of stress, which gradually lead to full Burn Out manifested as an onset of increased doubt, indecisiveness, and definitely a loss of humour. Where only a few weeks before I was a strong leader, I now couldn't face going to work!

**Physiological Symptoms of Stress**

- Insomnia
- Increased onset of headaches
- Ritualistic wakening at 1am to 3am
- Fatigue
- Fluctuating body temperature
- Lowered Libido
- Decreased immunity
- Hormonal Imbalance
- Diarrhea or constipation
- Lowered natural production of serotonin
- Increased production of cortisol
- Increased resting heart rate
- Skin changes (rashes, itchiness or dryness)
- Dryness of mouth or throat
- Shallow breathing or shortness of breath
- Reduced ability to burn fat

These symptoms then promote behavioural changes, which then cause us to spiral into a never-ending loop.

Your thoughts – Impact your actions – which impact the outcome – which impact your beliefs – which impact your thoughts…

Choose now NOT to pass the blame to others or to your environment. Take responsibility that you yourself let this eventuate, and do something about it!

Stress is an immediate signal, a wake-up call if you will - that change is necessary.

## Biology further explained

Although your body has 11 systems within it that pull the wheels and turn the cogs (such as the digestive and circulatory systems), there are two PIVOTAL systems that play a major role in your Immunity and Inner Health and are impacted by Stress directly.

These are the Nervous System and the Endocrine System.

The Nervous System (NS) is responsible for sending, receiving and processing nerve impulses throughout your body. It is made up of your brain, spinal cord, sensory organs, and all of the nerves that connect these organs with the rest of the body.

The brain and spinal cord make up the Central Nervous System (CNS), which carries neural messages from the brain to the rest of the body. From the spinal cord, the Peripheral Nervous System (PNS) connects the CNS to the rest of the body's limbs. Running parallel to the CNS and PNS, the Autonomic Nervous System (ANS) is the one that controls our life support systems such as blood circulation, food digestion, and breathing. It is the ANS that is entirely run subconsciously.

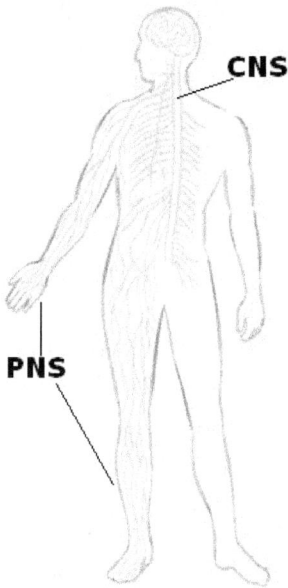

*Central Nervous System (CNS) and Peripheral Nervous System (PNS)*

In short, your brain is linked to every other part of your body by a myriad of highways and vice versa.

When the brain perceives an outside threat to be real (through your thoughts and perceptions), it changes the neural messaging to the ANS, telling it to speed up or slow down functions within the body. During acute stress, your ANS tells your digestive system to effectively shut down, telling the gut that it doesn't need to actively break down the food because there are more important functions to worry about.

Hence often when we've been under attack from stress for some time, we start to pile on the kilos or get a sudden onset of diarrhea with no obvious cause.

When faced with an imminent danger, it is your nervous system that gives you an <u>instant</u> response (as opposed to your endocrine system); it activates quickly and allows you to jump out of the way of an oncoming car without a second thought.

All in all, our bodies are doing amazing things all the time, yet this is where we throw a spanner in the works and set up a kill switch - what I call the Stress Lever.

The Endocrine System (ES) is the slower responder of the two. It includes all the glands of the body and the hormones produced by those glands. By regulating the functions of organs in the body these glands help to maintain the body's hormonal homeostasis (balance).

Chronic stress that wears you down over time directly impacts the Adrenal glands (within the ES) until eventually they effectively run out of steam and stop producing sufficient hormones – basically they get tired.


Your ES is controlled by neural commands from your NS (your brain, being the central command).

Remember that your nervous system is where your FAST acting responses occur.

The "Fight or flight" adrenal (ES) response kicks in only AFTER you've jumped out of the way of the oncoming car, to use the same metaphor.

Your Adrenal Medulla (which sit atop your kidneys) controls the production of Epinephrine (otherwise known as adrenalin), which courses through your circulatory system, binding to proteins on the sides of cells throughout your body.

When it binds to the wall of the liver, it sends neural intent to cells inside the liver to convert Glycogen to Glucose, which is then instantly released into the blood stream – effectively giving you a sugar rush.

That 'sugar rush' causes your breathing rate to increase, your heart beat to speed up and your arteries to dilate which sends more blood to the muscles to give you momentary bouts of strength (hence why you've probably heard of people lifting cars when they have an intense adrenalin rush). When our bodies enter into the Fight or Flight response, our brain tells other "less important" organs and glands to slow down or redirect so our body can concentrate on survival.

Consider what would happen if you were the victim of constant stressor attacks. Your body would be overloaded with epinephrine, great. But, the downside of this is that when one hormone is spiked for too long, another usually suffers.

1. Our digestive system slows, meaning if we continue to eat our usual diet during this time, we could find our weight increases.

2. Blood is shunted away from the heart and toward our extremities, which is why we have sudden bursts of strength. Imagine the toll on the heart if it continues in this fashion though…

3.  Hormone productivity is slowed or stopped all together.  For example, your body responds by dropping its levels of progesterone and estrogen to ensure you don't fall pregnant during this "attack".

4.  The Probiotics in the villi within your digestive tract are altered, causing gastro problems such as diarrhea or Irritable Bowel Syndrome (IBS).

5.  And your body ramps up its production of inflammatory cells, causing you to be more prone to aches and pains (hence you wake up one morning with a sore neck for no reason at all).

As part of this Fight or Flight response your Adrenal Cortex produces another hormone called Cortisol (also known as the 'stress hormone'. These hormones are created naturally throughout the day at precise times and durations.  It is only when our environment and brain interfere with these cycles that we become imbalanced.   We go against the flow, we swim upstream and we wonder why we get so tired.

Cortisol naturally begins production from about 5am every morning, giving you access to ENERGY as you wake up.  Although termed the 'stress hormone', its production is an essential element in our body's life cycle.  By 11am, it has reached its peak production and will slowly reduce throughout the rest of the day.

Imagine if your brain thought you were still at risk of being in harms way and therefore continued to release cortisol and epinephrine every day, all day for months or years at a time?  **Sadly this scenario is becoming all too common and is why we're seeing a rise in both stress leave and diagnoses of depression.**

Effectively you've interfered with your body's natural biorhythms.  2 of the spokes on your wheel are now longer than all the others, and thus the wheel can no longer turn.

Cortisol production is a good thing.  Too much cortisol production is a problem.

I myself went 7 full nights without an ounce of sleep.  I had thought this was physically and mentally impossible until I experienced it.  I knew this was considered a form of torture in many cultures, but with the levels of cortisol and adrenalin in my body, my brain had no way of knowing I needed to sleep.  Torture works when your brain knows it needs to sleep but is not *allowed* to.  I lay there night after night counting sheep, until sleeplessness also became a habit that was hard to break.

Once I knew what to do, it took a full 3 weeks to fall back into a nice slumber habit once more and I forced myself to realise that even a 10-minute nap was a win for me during that time.

I also realized that just like weight loss, the longer you stay slumped at the bottom of the hill trying to find a way back up, the longer it will take to climb back up to the top again.  Please don't wait until you've experienced burn

out or anxiety to take control.  Know your triggers and
start rebooting now.

Luckily for us all, there is a way back to normal
hormonal regulation without the need for medical
intervention or hormone replacement therapy.

## The gist...

A person's natural tendency (from infancy) is NOT to be
a "night owl" but to be a "Lark".  We become night owls
through religious habits in our late teens (partying until
the wee small hours and sleeping in late – ring any
bells?).

Being a night owl may seem natural to some of you (such as those who work night shifts, or play in a band); however, over time you suppress your body's natural biorhythms that allow for balanced hormone production. You effectively shut down your body's natural alarm clock (circadian and ultradian rhythms), and your endocrine system becomes confused.

Everything in life follows some form of cycle. There is a continual flow of some kind in everything we see. There would be no night without day. Life as we know it would not exist if there was no gravitational pull. The tide would not ebb without its flow, and the earth would not spin without the pull from the moon and the sun.

**The human body should sleep when it is dark and move about when it is light. Simple.**

During normal cycles, when darkness hits your retina (your eye), your hypothalamus sends messages around your body, which eventually reach your pineal gland via your sympathetic nervous system (SNS). Your pineal gland then secretes melatonin, which slows your heart rate and 'gets you ready for sleep".

No darkness = No natural production of melatonin.

No melatonin = no natural onset of sleepiness.

If we remain on "high alert" through ongoing stress, the ES continues to produce cortisol. It is only when cortisol is depleted during the night that serotonin (your "calm" hormone) is produced (usually at 1am during deep sleep). If your cortisol levels aren't given the chance or signal to drop, or if your body has forgotten to kick-start the production of Melatonin (think Night Shift), your body will stop producing serotonin. You will then miss out on having the natural ability to feel CALM!

To recap; no melatonin = inability to get to sleep, then no serotonin production = waking up frazzled and fried. Not a great cocktail thus far...

You now have every excuse in the book to snap at your kids, right?

Could this be a 'Light Bulb' moment for you?

Sadly the bad news doesn't stop there.

High levels of cortisol also raise the body's prolactin levels meaning you gain a heightened sense of **pain,** perhaps in the form of a stiff neck, or muscle aches.

Where once long ago you could fall asleep effortlessly and could sleep through anything (remember your teens!), now days your mind and body are seemingly fighting against you in every possible way.

I'm already getting tired just writing about this! And yet, I can bet that many of you reading this are nodding your head with full understanding.

**Stress impacts our sleep. Sleep impacts our health**.

The two are tightly bound together and should be worked on as a team.

And to make matters worse, we then suffer decreased dopamine levels in the brain (another symptom of sleep deprivation), which then reduces our ability to experience FUN, which causes a further knock on effect of reduced Oxytocin in our system (our love hormone), and you've now got a toxic cocktail that can kill.

Knock, Knock - Welcome anxiety and depression.

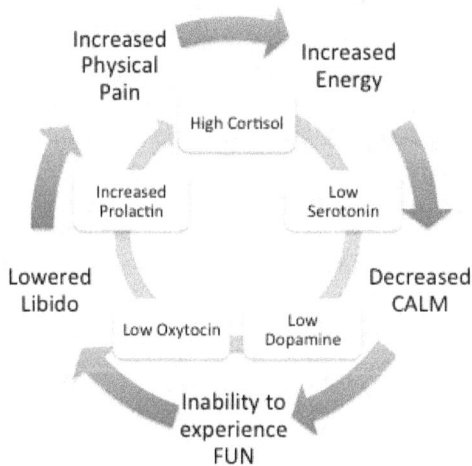

Increased Physical Pain

Increased Energy

High Cortisol

Increased Prolactin

Low Serotonin

Lowered Libido

Decreased CALM

Low Oxytocin

Low Dopamine

Inability to experience FUN

*The vicious cycle of Stress, Sleep and Hormones*

You need sleep to balance your hormones, but you need to reduce your stress to enable regenerative sleep. It's a vicious cycle.  Add to this your tendency to stay up late, and you've effectively cut your body's ultradian rhythm in half, meaning you never reach the cycle of sleep needed to produce serotonin.  Screaming kids *will* get louder, the dirty laundry *will* seem overwhelming, the traffic *will* become the bane of your life, and your libido… well, what libido?

I love the analogy that Stephen Covey uses when he artfully tells the story of a Woodcutter whose saw gets progressively blunter as time passes as he continues to cut down trees.
If the woodcutter were to stop sawing to sharpen his saw, he would actually save tie and effort in the long run.  Most of us are like the woodcutter.  Firstly its hard to see the wood for the massive piles of trees in front of us, but we harbor on and get so buried in the problems that we fail to stop and pay attention to the real cause of our emotional downfall.

## OK, so HOW DO I fix this??

Most people don't really care about the research and the scientific facts that are outlined in this book.  And to be honest, this "how do I fix this" question is the reason I started writing this book in the first place.  There is so much information out there, but we seem to have little or no time to sit down and reflect upon it all.  We just want to know what to do and not spend days searching for the answers.

Many people actually think they are good sleepers, yet can't understand why they too seem to become easily irritated. You may THINK you sleep well, but many of us fall asleep easily yet are unable to reach the deep sleep that is required for repair.

I learnt the art of getting straight to the point years ago in my corporate life. I would be told time and time again from my stakeholders and sponsors "don't waste my valuable time, tell me what's wrong and how to fix it!"

And seriously, although right now everything may seem overwhelming and the more your read the more your mind boggles; following the steps and stages outlined in this book REALLY IS VERY SIMPLE and life changing.

You could spend hundreds of dollars seeing counselors, psychologists or life coaches who will assist you on your journey to reduce stress in your life. As long as you resonate with the person who is guiding you, you will have a good chance at beating your demons through solid practice and discipline.

But why spend the money when all you need to know is already within your own mind? You've simply lodged it away and forgotten where to find the key to unlock the memory.

When I first suffered from a severe bout of Stress Burn Out, I left my partner for 2 weeks, and did everything I could to de-stress. I practiced yoga daily, went to a psychologist, turned off the TV, practiced my 4A's (Avoid, alter, accept, adapt), changed my thought patterns, read relaxing books, and went for solitary walks in the local forest to feel at one with nature every day. After two weeks, I felt I was then ready and able to go back to my life, my routines and my partner. And I did well, for many years, until 3 years later I once again "forgot" how to cope.

Here's the moral of this story: You can do all the usual stress management practices in the world, and believe me, I tried them all, but if within you, you carry ANY of the following beliefs (go on, put your hand up!) then your life can't help but take you down the same spiral staircase over and over again.

"Your wish is your command".

- I have a strong work ethic.
- I don't entirely trust that anyone else can do 'this' as fast or as well as I can
- I am everything to my kids; my husband comes in a clear second place
- I need to work harder in order to keep my job and make money
- I'm married to a schmuck. If I don't pick up after him, the house would be a total mess!
- My list of things to do is growing daily, and I don't have enough time in the day for myself
- If I can just get through the next few years until the kids are older, I'll then be able to reclaim some time for myself
- My partner/child/mother is sick, and I have to be the one to support them and provide
- I'm programmed this way through strong family values

Just to prompt a little thought pattern into your brain before I go on; is there room for YOU in any of the beliefs above?

Yes, yes I know. We've all chosen to be the best we can be. But here's my question to you...

If you were to drop dead tomorrow (please don't take that the wrong way!), would those around you eventually cope without you? And would they remember you for being the "fun loving, joyous, and laughing" person that you wanted to be, or do you think they would say, "Oh thank goodness she/he cleaned up after me all that time! I'm so glad he/she gave up their better years of fun to work so hard on my behalf".

So?

If you do anything at all from now on, please honour me this: You are not on this earth to be sad or stressed. You WILL miss out on living your life if you carry on in the same manner. Life is meant to be enjoyed. It is meant to be honoured. Your body and brain are so much more than you give it credit for being, so don't just sit there and take it!

# TAKE IT BACK!

Remember what it felt like when you first fell in love? Your body was flooded with Oxytocin, meaning you felt awesome and had loads of energy. You were happy, time passed too quickly, and your senses were on high alert for wonderful experiences. Do you recall *ever* being sick when you first fell in love? No! Because your brain was on overdrive! It was flooding your body with those beautiful chemicals. There was no room in your brain for negative influencers.

The same is true when you see a puppy or baby. Your internal levels of DHEA rise in order to balance your hormones, your heart rate and blood pressure normalize and the production of the stress hormone Cortisol decreases. All in the blink of an eye, purely from witnessing the feelings of being close to a puppy, baby or just by being in love!

There are hundreds of techniques for stress relief and hundreds more for stress management. The list below outlines some of the easiest and most obvious of these techniques. The fastest way to build resiliency in your life toward stress, anxiety and depression is to seek out FUN and find LOVE.

## Stress Management Techniques

1. Avoid Excess Stressors - Turn off all negative influences, such as Television, radio, and negative people thereby reducing the amplified attack. You just don't need the excessive inputs!

2. Breathing Exercises- if you feel suddenly overwhelmed, excuse yourself, go to the

bathroom, close your eyes and practice conscious breathing. Slowly breathe in through your nose for a count of 4, and out through either your mouth or nose for a count of 6. Picture the air travel through your nostrils and into your lungs to effectively distract your thoughts. If you're in public, there is no need to close your eyes; you can perform breathing exercises anywhere! There is no excuse!

3. Remember to activate the Right side of you brain (where the Calm influence resides) by blocking your right nostril and breathing in through your left nostril only.

4. Drink Green Tea – L-Theanine, an active ingredient, is an amino acid found in tea plants that promotes relaxation.

5. Listen to music - As with the puppy scenario, if you listen to uplifting music your DHEA production increases.

6. Exercise - When you exercise

   - Noradrenaline is released which helps to relieve depression.
   - Endorphines are released giving you a feeling of calm and wellbeing
   - Blood circulation improves
   - Digestive function improves
   - Sleep is deeper and more regenerative

7. Remove clutter from your life. Research suggests that clutter in your home can contribute to clutter in your mind. Is now a good time for a garage sale?

8. Get a massage – not only relaxing, but this simple act promotes healthy blood circulation and a feeling of well being

9. Activate all your senses. Smell (aromatherapy). Sight (Watch a funny movie). Taste (eat healthy but glorious foods). Sound (Listen to uplifting music). Touch (Get a massage, or pat a puppy)

10. Create a friendship circle or plan new social events. Social gatherings allow for increased energy and feelings of community and love

11. Meditation – Oh the benefits of meditation. I could go on for hours. It helps to lower blood pressure, calm your mind, slow your heart rate, and has even been linked to living a longer life! AND there is now scientific evidence to support all of these claims! Hallelujah.

12. Remove nutritional stressors from your diet, such as alcohol, caffeine, recreational drugs, sugar and high fats, where you can.

13. Practice being more of a witness and less involved in what is going on around you.

14. Smile as much as you can, even if you don't mean it. Fake it.

15. Start a journal. When you place your thoughts onto paper, your brain accepts that the stressor has been dealt with and parks it away for the mean time.

16. Write down your "To Do" list before heading to the bedroom to avoid getting that racing mind in the middle of the night. Even if you never get back to the list, your mind feels safer is something is written down.

17. Ensure you get your 7.5 hours of restful sleep each night.

18. Reframe your thoughts. Start seeing your problems from a different point of view and try to look for the opportunity or message in every hurdle.

And DO try the WOF Challenge outlined in the DIY Bible later in this book.

I hope to see you in the gap with a smile on your face.

*"For the human mind is seldom at stay: if you do not grow better, you will most undoubtedly grow worse"* – *Samuel Richardson*

# Chapter Five – The power of your MIND

Your subconscious mind helps you get through the day and runs your life. It drives the car without you having to be actively involved. It takes you for a walk without your conscious concentration on how to place one foot in front of the other. And for many of us, you're paid for work you perform at your workplace where often you "could do it in your sleep". For all of the above activities our subconscious takes over most of the "doing" and allows you to remain consciously aware of what else is around you. Invariably you learnt each of these activities through repetition. You weren't born knowing how to drive a car, or to walk for that matter. But you learnt through trial and error and soon, through ensuring the action became a habit, it was engrained in your subconscious.

The exact same principle is true for how we form beliefs. Take a kitten away from its mother when it is born and place it in a kennel with a dog; that kitten will grow up thinking it too is a dog and take on many of the characteristics of its canine mother.

Similarly (and well proven in research studies around the world) take a child from one country and adopt it into a family that has a strong genetic link to Cancer, and by the time that child matures he/she also has adopted the genetic disposition as inherited through the belief of family ties.

Did you know that by your 18th birthday, you have been told "No you can't" over 184,000 times! What do you think that does to your beliefs about your self worth?

Up to the age of 7 years old, we are assimilating information from our environment and the people around us to form our subconscious beliefs and thought patterns that take us through to adulthood. Once you turn 7, your foundation beliefs are engrained and your subconscious thoughts take over 90% of your daily activity and patterns, leaving only 10% of those 80,000 thoughts a day within your control. If you're a parent with young children, know that you do have the power to change the habits and beliefs of your children now.

So how do you change beliefs that have been with you since you were 7 if they are locked deep within your subconscious?

A common method is to perform hypnosis where effectively the patient is made to relax completely, let down their guard and let somebody else plant suggestive intentions into their mind. For many, this process may work wonders. For others however, hypnosis doesn't seem to work. Why?

Hypnosis works when you fully and completely let go and trust the hypnotist. For some people, the thought of being helpless for even just a moment incites fear and invariably the mind closes the door to any subconscious "attack" without us being aware that it is happening.

So, the question once more remains; HOW do you change your beliefs in order to *Heal and Lead a Stress Free Life*?

…By forming and creating a HABIT by the use of FOCUS.

**Your brain will help you if you tell it what to do.**

I love to recount to my audience a "trick" that Jack Canfield uses in his seminars. And I hope with his permission that I can share this little trick with you here. It is a perfect way to show you how powerful your mind really is.

Try this now.

On the base of each of your palms are 2 crease lines that have been formed from years of folding your hands forwards and backwards.

Find these 2 lines now on each hand. Carefully bring your wrists together so that each line connects with its corresponding line on the other wrist.

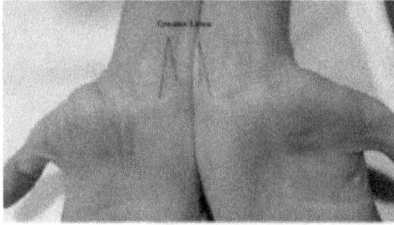

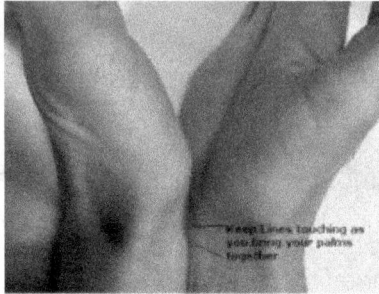

Now, with all 4 lines touching, bring your palms and fingers together in the prayer position. Notice now whether one hand seems a little shorter than the other? (Ignore nail length ladies!).

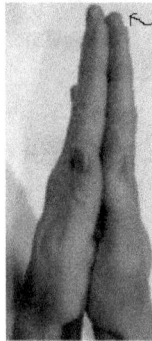

Leave the shorter hand where it is, dropping your longer hand out of the way. Concentrate on that shorter hand. Focus on it and now say 8x with intent (meaning you really, really, really want this to happen);

"Grow longer"

8x I said!

Now do the same test again, finding the creases, bringing them together and back into the prayer position. Are your hands now the same length?

Cool huh!?

Your focus, along with your neural intent, meant you couldn't lose. Your hand HAD to lengthen. The same principle applies to both your mental health, and your physical health. What you focus on expands. "This arthritis is killing me" – and so it is. "I have awful eyesight" – and so it is. "I'll always suffer from back pain because…" and so it is.

Change your story! Change it now, and don't believe a word of what you've been telling yourself, or have been told by others over the years. You can do anything you set your mind to. And by the way, yes, your hand will return back to its natural length now that you're no longer focusing consistently on its growth.

On another note;

Have you ever looked down and noticed a small nick in your skin that suddenly bled once you looked at it? Perhaps that same lesion was there since the morning when you were shaving but you never noticed it before, however now you can't control the volume of blood rushing out of this small wound? Your attention caused that lesion to bleed.

Did you ever wonder why acne always appears just before a big date or presentation? Yes we know acne can be caused by stress, but it's actually our worry about how we will look on the day that sparks our body into action. "Please, please, please, do NOT break out on May 4th!" – and so it is.

## Affirmations

To many, practicing affirmations (which is the art of saying a positive sentence many times throughout the day) sounds like 'mumbo-jumbo'. However, think back on how you learnt to write or spell when you were at school. You did so by repetition. The word "hospital" didn't come easily for many 5 year olds learning to spell for the first time, but we got there in the end, didn't we? The art form of practicing affirmations has been proven to slowly change the neural pathways in your brain (neuroplasticity). After a while, the statement is so natural that it rolls off your tongue effortlessly, and sits deep within your subconscious as a new belief.

If your affirmation is the polar opposite to your current reality, your subconscious has to decide which reality to believe.  The more you say something; the more it becomes your reality.  Hence the common saying:

"Fake it till you make it"

If you want to stop doing something that is a habit, you don't just stop suddenly.  Crazy I know!  But to successfully quit something, for example biting your nails, you must first replace that habit with something new, else find yourself right back where you started again a few months later.  Each time you think about biting your nails, you must instantly think about or reach for something different like sugar-free gum.  Do this thought replacement process religiously for 3 weeks, and your addiction to biting your nails will have disappeared entirely.   The same is true for losing weight.  Yes you can change your diet, but unless you change your habits your weight will continue to pile back on year after year, diet after diet.

If you feel stressed by being in enclosed places, begin building resilience to that stressor by saying daily affirmations that you 'love enclosed spaces – they make you feel so happy' whilst imagining yourself in that small space feeling calm and relaxed.

If you fear something, the saying "Face your fears" is wholly appropriate.  Ideally you are replacing your fear with a new appreciation of the item or situation.  The more you do it, the less the fear, so don't expect to be fearless in the face of sharks after only one dive for example.

To be frank, the art of affirmations is not in my 6 step DIY bible, but I firmly believe it works wonders and should be taught in schools to build self confidence.

The art of controlling your thoughts is covered in more detail in the Stress Management Techniques chapter later in this book.

## The Brain - 101

The human brain is a complex organ that produces electrical signals, which together with chemical reactions, controls all neural activity in your body. The average human brain weighs just 3 pounds (1300-1400g) once it is fully formed by the age of 6 years. I would love to quiz "our maker" when I see him/her as to why our noses and ears continue to grow throughout our lives, when our brain's remain so static. It seems paradoxical to me! Nonetheless; your brain uses 20% of your oxygen supply and 20% of the body's blood flow.

If a person weighs 62kg for example, their brain constitutes only 2.2% of their total body weight, yet it uses a quarter of its blood and oxygen. If your heart were to separate from your body, it would continue to beat until it ran out of oxygen (up to an hour). Your brain however would run out of oxygen within only a few short minutes (anywhere between 1.5 and 3 minutes).

Your brain needs a LOT of Oxygen in order to maintain optimal state and flow. When was the last time you stopped and took a deep long breath, preferably through your nose to ensure that oxygen makes a direct path to your brains supply?

Your brain is made up of many parts. The most important areas that relate to this subject are outlined here.

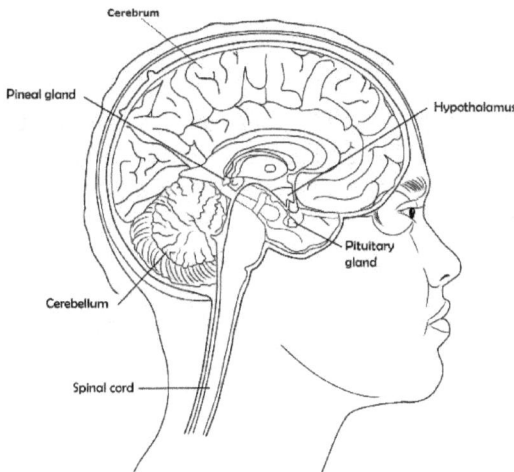

1.  Cerebrum

Your Cerebrum is the largest mass of your brain, taking up over 85% of the brains weight. It is known as the "thinking" part of the brain. It controls memory, muscle movement, sensation, judgment, and reason. In order to solve a puzzle or your math equation, it is your cerebrum that is at work.

The cerebrum can be divided into two exact halves, with a line running down the central path of the human head from the front to the back, effectively creating a LEFT and RIGHT brain.

The RIGHT side of the brain activates when you are performing **creative** or abstract tasks, such as drawing, designing, creating music, or thinking of colours.

The LEFT side of the brain activates when the task at hand is more ANALYTICAL, such as when solving a complex problem, doing math, using logic, or creating 'to do' lists.

Research tells us that most people develop deeper, stronger neural pathways on one side of the cerebrum, depending on whether they resonate to a factual, analytical identity or a creative, heart centered identity.

What is interesting though is that as the cerebrum also activates the use of your muscles, they do so by controlling the muscles on the OPPOSITE side of the body.  In counter, as the nasal passageways are directly connected to the brain, you can activate the impulses and energy on the opposite side of the brain, just by closing off one nostril and breathing slowly.

In essence, by breathing through your left nostril only, you are able to activate the calming, creative side of your brain (the right side), thereby gaining an immediate relief from stress!

I trust you've just tried this as you were reading, yes?

You can also tell what type of "thinker" you are by performing a similar test:

Concentrate on your breathing and over the next minute, notice whether one nostril seems to feel freer that the other. Perhaps you will notice that you are slightly stuffy in your right side, or the air seems colder through your left? If you felt an easier pathway through your left nasal passage, then you are generally a RIGHT brained thinker (more creative).

If you felt an easier pathway through your right nasal passage, then you have a tendency for LEFT brained thinking (more analytical). Children may find they are equally free through both nostrils as they have yet to feel the pull of society to challenge their analytical mind (at school or at work), and sometimes you may find your right nasal passage opens when you're at work, but the opposite is true once you relax at home if intrinsically you know you're a creative soul.

Your cerebrum also does an amazing trick every 90 minutes by **switching electrical activity to the opposite side of your brain for 20 minutes!**

What this means is that if you have been concentrating hard on a project for 90 minutes (using your analytical brain), you would do well to take a 20 minute break and do something creative. This doesn't mean you have to stop what you are doing; it simply means that you should change your focus. Perhaps start designing the *diagrams* of that same project for example.

Have you ever spent 8 hours staring at a computer screen working on ONE excel spreadsheet and come home feeling a little like a squashed vegetable? If only you had changed your focus every 90 minutes, your brain wouldn't have struggled to maintain its focus and you would have finished your day feeling entirely different, refreshed even.

If you work from home, these 90 minute mini-breaks are the optimal time to schedule in your housekeeping chores. If you schedule them in this way, they tend to feel less like chores and more like achievements.

2. The Brain Stem

Your brain stem is the messenger of all neural intent in your body. It is the controller of all of our involuntary muscles (such as your stomach and heart). It also sorts through the millions of messages that the brain and the rest of the body send back and forth. Drugs such as Opiates work to alleviate pain responses by stopping the neural transmission through the brain stem.

3. The Limbic System

The Limbic system is made up of three structures; the amygdala, the hippocampus, and the hypothalamus. Together these 3 structures are responsible for all your **emotions**. They enable us to show affection, fall in love, form friendships and even alter expressions of mood. It is the Limbic system, specifically the hypothalamus that enables us to laugh.

So the next time someone tells you "It's all in your mind", agree with them! It is!

Once you understand how simple your brain make-up *really* is, how it is a system of On/Off codes being sent around your body, you then have the ability to change what your brain is telling your body to do.

You can reactivate the synaptic flow to one area of your body by purely **concentrating on that area** or applying pressure along the neural pathway (reflexology / acupressure).

You can unblock constriction, increase blood flow, and increase the energy flow to any area of your body to advance your healing.

Consider the topic of Neuroplasticity, which is the brains ability to change and adapt as a result of learning. The brains *physical* makeup can change, depending on your thoughts and environment.

Functional Plasticity refers to the brain's ability to move functions from a damaged area of the brain to other undamaged areas (basically giving a brain cell a different job)

Structural Plasticity refers to the brain's ability to actually change its physical structure as a result of learning or meditation.

If the physical pathways in your brain can reform, then surely there is hope for you yet!

*"Change your story. Make every story a love story"* – *Deepak Chopra*

## Your Challenge

I would hope that by now you've come to understand how amazing you really are. You should be so enlightened at this point that you are up for a challenge, no?

Ok, so let's make it an easy challenge to start you off. But let's make sure this is something that will assist the shift in your subconscious belief system too.

I am going to ask you to perform a 'kind' of meditation, or visual exercise. This is so easy that once you've accomplished this, you could invite your friends or kids to try it out too!

So, without further ado, find yourself a comfortable space where you feel safe from interruption and peer ridicule (!). Find a sitting position that feels comfortable to you and close your eyes (read this first! I'm not THAT awesome! Or you can download the audio from www.thehealthhug.com)

Pay conscious attention to your breath.

With your eyes closed, count your breath intake (in for 4 counts)

Hold briefly.

Exhale whilst counting for 6 counts.

Consciously breathe in and out 6 times whilst your body relaxes and your mind slows.

When you feel peaceful, bring your attention to the area of your heart.

FEEL your heart beat. If you can't feel it, place your hand gently over your heart until you do. You may also find it easier if you breathe in, and hold your breath for this first "find mission". There is no rush.

Once you are fully aware of your heartbeat, concentrate on it until it grows stronger. Breathe naturally.

Now set your intention (think) on moving that heart beat up your body, over toward your arm, and down toward your fingers. You may need to do this more than once to "get it".

Feel the beat move, and witness as your intention begins a new sensation in your hands or fingers. Do not think about anything else.

You may feel warmth; tingling or a strong beat in your fingers.

Notice it, feel it and slowly open your eyes.


What did you just do?!!


You used the power of your mind to send neural messaging towards an area of your body. You can do this 'trick' on any limb or organ. This little exercise is helpful if you want to tell your brain to start healing an area that brings you pain.


Note; if this didn't work for you, try it again when you are feeling more relaxed, or take more time on the initial breathing exercise. If your mind is filled with other thoughts, it will not have the power needed for this intention.


Once you have successfully achieved this task once, it will become easier for you each time.

Hopefully you're starting to understand the power that your thoughts and mind have over the functions and symptoms within your physical body.

Your thoughts control your hormone production, neurochemical production, whether you feel pain or not, and also tell the body how to respond to certain stressors. Nausea, constipation, sweating, body rashes, diarrhea, acid reflux, bowel issues - these are all signs manifested by your body to ask you to stop and pay attention.

What is your body trying to tell you?

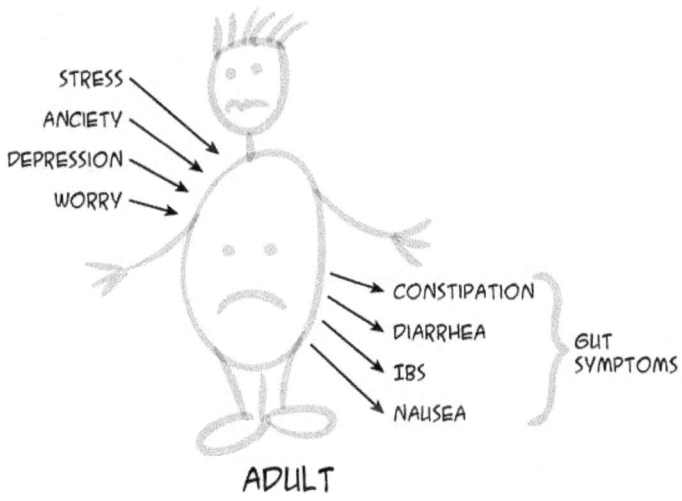

STRESS
ANCIETY
DEPRESSION
WORRY

CONSTIPATION
DIARRHEA
IBS
NAUSEA

GUT SYMPTOMS

ADULT

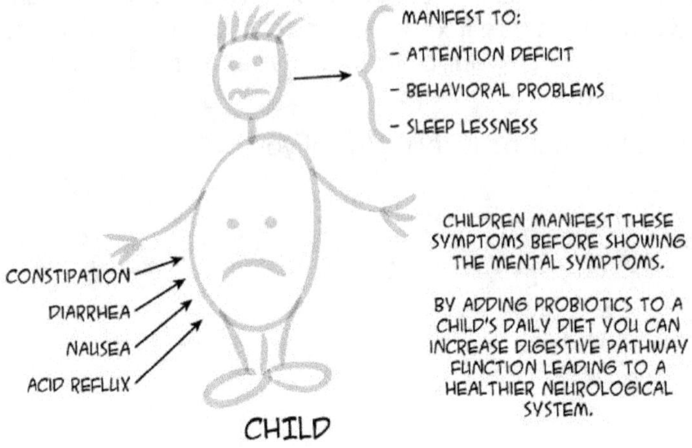
MANIFEST TO:
- ATTENTION DEFICIT
- BEHAVIORAL PROBLEMS
- SLEEP LESSNESS
CHILDREN MANIFEST THESE SYMPTOMS BEFORE SHOWING THE MENTAL SYMPTOMS.
BY ADDING PROBIOTICS TO A CHILD'S DAILY DIET YOU CAN INCREASE DIGESTIVE PATHWAY FUNCTION LEADING TO A HEALTHIER NEUROLOGICAL SYSTEM.
CONSTIPATION
DIARRHEA
NAUSEA
ACID REFLUX
CHILD

Now let's continue to blow your mind…

---

"I will love the light for it shows me the way, yet I will endure the darkness for it shows me the stars."
— Og Mandino

---

# Chapter Six - Laughter

This is such an important chapter, and yet I doubt I could do it justice. With so many research studies flooding in, it is impossible to ignore the evidence that clearly shows the importance of Laughter in healing. The sad state of adulthood though is that we no longer seek out the fun that we used to as children. Back then we laughed an average of 400 times a day.

Counter this with the average that an adult laughs in any given day, which is between 12-14 times, and you have to wonder why we were so quick to forget how much fun it can be. Once again, we let the pressures of life and the social beliefs of others stop us from experiencing one of or God-given birthrights - to have fun whilst experiencing all that this earth life has to offer.

And as described earlier, without laughter, our feel good chemicals in the brain are reduced. As they reduce, we feel less inclined to laughter. Again, a vicious cycle.

I can remember having a full 2 years where the thought of anyone laughing made me jealous. I wanted to be able to laugh, but I had so little of the good chemicals left in my brain that I was running on empty. I went to see fun movies and walked out unimpressed. I paid the big ticket dollars to see International Comedians on tour, and was frustrated that when everyone else around me were in hysterics, I was suffering with a small smile.

Instead of laughing when my children did something cute or wonderful, I was on the brink of tears. Laughter does not always come easy for many of us. I get that; but laughter does return if you allow it to. The first step is to acknowledge that Laughter is perhaps the greatest goal you could work towards on any given day, and set everything else aside for a while until you achieve it. For me, the laughter slowly came back after I'd mastered the art of stress resilience, after I had inner peace. But what was most interesting was that although laughter was the last to return, my inner smile was growing daily, meaning that when the laughter did come, it came in waves!

Laughter really is the best medicine;

1. When we laugh, our count of natural Killer cells, (such as T-cells, B-Cells and Gamma-Interferon), increases.

2. Laughter also dampens the production of stress hormones such as Cortisol.

3. Laughter increases the concentration of salivary immunoglobin A, which defends against infectious organisms entering through the respiratory tract (thereby saving you from contracting that Flu that's been going around your office). It's a common response in my family that when a child starts coughing, they are instantly prescribed a dose of tickle monsters to make them laugh!

4. It is estimated that laughing 100x is equal to 10 mins on the rowing machine, or 15 mins on an exercise bike. Laughing gives your diaphragm and abdominal, respiratory, facial, leg and back muscles a full work out.

5. It lowers your blood pressure

6. It increases blood flow and oxygenation of the blood which assists healing

7. Laughter has now been credited with being as powerful as some opiate drugs in the relief of pain. It is said that 15 mins of belly aching laughter can give a patient up to 2 hours of pain relief.

On Albert Einstein's deathbed, he said that there was only one thing he regretted in his life; his lack of playtime.

So ask yourself; when was the last time you truly laughed? Laughing gently throughout the day just doesn't cut it. I mean BELLY ACHING LAUGHTER. If there is only one thing you take from this book today, please let it be this:

Seek fun and laughter and ensure you laugh AS MUCH AS YOU CAN throughout the rest of your life.

The human race often forgets to have fun. We concentrate on getting something done, and suddenly 3 weeks have gone by and we're feeling less than optimal. Ensure FUN is scheduled in your diary in advance, so you don't fall into this trap.

If your child is coming down with a cold, stop it dead in its tracks by piling fun and laughter into their day. The more giggling and laughing you hear, the faster the healing process. Believe me, tickling really is the best option!

---

*I've always thought that a big laugh is a really loud noise from the soul saying, "Ain't that the truth." ~Quincy Jones*

---

# Chapter Seven - SLEEP

Sleep is the one and only time in the 24-hour day that our body has the ability to heal itself. So when I hear people saying that they have no need for sleep, or that they survive on less than 4 hours of sleep a night, I can't help but wonder what other ailments are starting to creep into their lives.

I think it's ironic that in a society so hell bent on finding the cure to many of man's diseases, that we are all still so ill-informed about the simple truth that sleep is THE MOST Important function in our lives.

"I have too much to do, there just isn't enough time to sleep!" is such a common phrase these days.

Human beings are supposed to be diurnal, meaning we sleep at NIGHT. Our body clocks are in synch with the moon and sun. Our energy hormones are at their optimal in the morning, and our relaxation hormones are highest in the evening.

Why mess with Mother Nature?

With the onset of night shifts, and the recent craving to party all night at your local bar, we are rapidly becoming a population of sleep-deprived zombies.

The longer you go without restful sleep, by waking intermittently, or reducing your sleep time in some way, the further into bad habit your sleep cycles go. If you were to tell me that you hadn't slept well in years, I could firmly state that your predicament was now part of your subconscious belief patterns.

This habit must be broken.

The pineal gland, located in your brain, secretes Melatonin, which is the chemical that promotes our circadian rhythms. When the sun goes down, your body is told to slow down. Fight against that by ingesting sugar or caffeine for instance, and your brain goes into a tailspin.

It's OK to defy nature for one or two nights, but to do so for months or even years on end is madness.

Sleep deprivation has been linked to:

1. Significant reductions in performance and alertness reducing your night time sleep by as little as one and a half hours for just one night could result in a reduction of daytime alertness by as much as 32%

2. High blood pressure

3. Heart attack

4. Heart failure

5. Stroke

6. Obesity

7. Psychiatric problems, including depression and other mood disorders

8. Attention Deficit Disorder (ADD)

9. Mental impairment

10. Fetal and childhood growth retardation

11. And even injury from accidents

The optimal sleep duration for an adult aged between 26 and 65 is 7.5 hours, reducing as we age, and is more for children (10hrs) and teens (8-9).

It is considered optimal to have fallen asleep by 10:30pm, and wake at 6am.

If you feel you need more sleep, have a nap in the early afternoon, instead of staying in bed until 10am so as not to impact your production of energy hormones. If you do stay in bed late in the morning, you waste your 'energy time zone' created by your natural cortisol spikes between 8 and 10am, meaning the rest of the waking day feels like a real chore on your energy levels.

# Techniques and Tools to aid the Onset of Sleep

1. If you are a night owl by habit, break this cycle by going to bed 10 minutes earlier every night for a period of 21 days. It takes 21-29 days to replace a habit remember! Stick with it!

2. Remove any blue light (such as alarm clocks) or technology (phones, televisions) from your bedroom. These DO interrupt your sleep patterns whether you believe it or not. Blue light is the one light colour that has been proven to permeate through your closed eyelids.

3. Refrain from partaking in alcohol, caffeine, or sugar after 2pm. I realise this one will be hard for many people! Think of this as a TEST that you are swatting hard for, and give yourself a gift at the end of those 21 days for all your hard efforts to make it more worthwhile for you. Caffeine for example, has a half life (for the average adult) of 5-7 hours. This means if you consume 200mg of caffeine at mid-day (being your average Latte), you would still have 100mg in your system at around 5.45pm, and 25% will still be in your system at 10pm. Do the math if you're an afternoon or dinnertime caffeine consumer!

4. If you have anything on your mind before you go to bed, write it down. This simple task relieves your mind as it gladly accepts the matter has been taken

care of for the time being.  Whether you action upon it the next day or not is irrelevant.

5.  Have a warm shower before bed.  The warm water is thought to warm the blood, which slows down the blood flow and improves our ability to relax.

6.  Do NOT take sleeping pills!  Although most sleeping pills help you to FALL asleep, they actually interfere with your sleep cycles once asleep.

7.  Add exercise to your daily routine.  The Endorphins produced are a natural sedative (after a few hours delay – don't try to fall into bed straight after an aggressive workout though).

8.  Have a cup of relaxing tea 30 minutes before bed, such as Chamomile.

9.  If you suffer from regular night waking, it is best to refrain from ingesting anything immediately before going to bed.  Eating can cause your digestion to kick into hyper-drive when it is supposed to be in slow-mode.  I've found this particularly true for women going into or through menopause.

10. Have a cup of warm milk.  When cows' milk is heated, a chemical reaction is created that forms an amino acid called Tryptophan. Tryptophan is

naturally formed in the human body to assist the creation of Serotonin, ensuring when you wake, you feel calmer.  The same amino is found in Turkey meat by the way.

11. If you wake in the night, do not turn the bright lights on to read.  Your brain still needs to know that it is nighttime, so if you get out of bed to read a book, please dim the lights, and do NOT watch an exciting movie, as this will only stimulate your brain.

## What can I do if I wake religiously during the night?

There are many reasons a person wakes during the night.  If you are a mother who is a light sleeper, any movement by your partner, any cry from your child, any purr from a cat can bring you out of deep slumber.  And really, when I say deep, I'm using this term loosely, as you've probably forgotten HOW to get to Phase 4 in your sleep cycle, which is the most restorative cycle for your body.

Remember that your subconscious holds tight to beliefs formed from habits after only 21 days?  Think about how long you've been forced to wake for your child, or snoring husband…perhaps this has been going on for years?  When you realize that your brain is waking you out of habit, you first must stop fighting it, or beating yourself up over it!  This is quite a natural occurrence and you share this nightly waking with hundreds of thousands of other people around the world.

But here's the good news.

You don't have to put up with it.

There are other causes, of course, for repetitive waking and each of these must be thoroughly eradicated for causal impact also. The fact that there are so many possible causes, may seem overwhelming to you, (which is something you are, of course trying to avoid in the first place!), however if you have all the facts, I think you'll find that ONE will jump out and hit you squarely between the eyes! You'll know instantly, "yes, that's me!"

If you know your sleep patterns are indeed a direct symptom of an external cause such as your childs constant cries, or your partners sleep movements (or snoring), ask your partner to help you out (if you can). Sleep in another room of the house for a few days or book yourself in to a motel just for a few nights to break the habit, or perhaps invest in a pair of effective noise cancelling earplugs. Tell your partner they've just inherited full waking parenting duties. And if they complain, ask them how much your mental health is worth to them!

If however you wake every night religiously at the same time with no known cause, perhaps you will relate to one of the following:

1. You struggle to fall asleep between 10pm and 11:30pm, and spend that time staring at the ceiling. High levels of cortisol are to blame (see

Chapter 8 for more details). Or you could have left over sugar or caffeine in your blood.

2. Do you wake between **1am and 3am** every morning, perhaps at the EXACT time each morning? (For me it was 1:04am for 6 weeks!).

Eastern medicine linked certain waking times to the activity of precise organs or processes in your body. Nutritionists around the Western world now fully endorse this prognosis, and having 'been there, done that' myself, I can attest that waking between 1-3am is a sure sign that your LIVER needs some TLC.

3. Do you wake some time **around 3am**, possibly feeling hungry or a bit jittery?

This can be due to a dramatic drop in blood sugar, and is usually a symptom of either a high carb diet, or a diet insufficient in nutrients. Your body will increase cortisol to break down valuable anabolic (tissue building) amino acids from protein to convert into glucose to elevate your blood sugar.

You may even lay awake for up to 2 hours tossing and turning and eventually fall asleep around 5am. If this sounds like you, please visit a nutritionist, and change your eating habits.

4.  You wake between **11pm and 1am**, or find if you get to bed too late, you won't be able to sleep until 1am anyway...?

According to the acupuncture meridian zones, this time period is associated with the gallbladder performing its regenerative functions. People impacted in this time slot are usually smokers, or people with too many bad fats in their diets.

5.  You wake religiously between **3am and 5am**, and often times with a stuffy nose.

3-5am is connected with your lungs and allergies. Allergies affecting the sinuses rear up at these times.

Here is a snapshot diagrammatic as an easier reference.

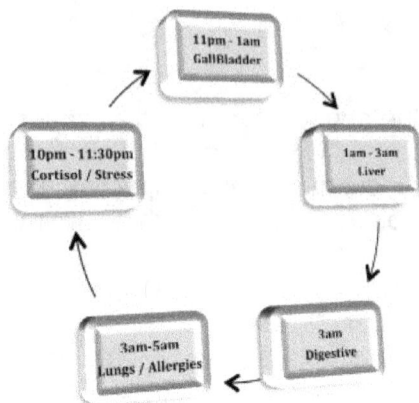

As you can see from the list above, MANY of our sleep problems are intrinsically linked to our diet. I cannot stress strongly enough the power of getting your eating habits under control. Invest in a nutritionist even for a single session to help you get more information and a clearer understanding.

Without QUALITY sleep, your body will

- Age prematurely

- Exacerbate aches and pains

- Lower your natural immunity

- Deplete your dopamine and serotonin levels

- Incur decreased ability to think clearly or heaven forbid, multi-task

…not to mention you'll look like death warmed up too!

Again, do not get frustrated if after the first week of changing your diet, or doing each of the steps in the first half of this chapter, you are still sleeping irregularly. Stick with it for 21 days, and see the power of this change!

You may need to ask your family to support you in this venture as it may impact them also (perhaps if you're trying to sleep whilst everyone else is still up watching loud movies for instance).

Another great tool is the art of reflexology as a sleep aid. Reflexology has been used for thousands of years by the French, Chinese and even Egyptians as a way to increase energy flow and blood circulation around the body. The Chinese use reflexology and Acupressure as an efficient natural form of analgesia in hospitals, and although disputed by modern medical society, the evidence to the effect and impact of this form of pain relief and neural activation is startling.

It works for me, so here's one of my favourites. Yes you can use reflexology on yourself, but for this simple technique to work its best with a partner. This technique is especially easy on children, and is so wonderful they can't wait to get in to bed with the promise of this foot massage.

Instructions:

The person lies on their back comfortably.  You position yourself at the end of their bed facing the base of their feet.

Hold the feet - one with each hand, thumb on the area at the top of the arch or base of the ball where there is a natural heart shape (see picture below) and fingers wrapped around the back of the foot, relaxed but holding onto the back of the feet.

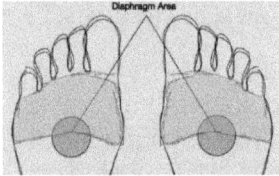

Diaphragm Area

Ask the person lying down to breath deeply in- and to try and breath into their stomach - if the stomach rises and falls they are breathing through their stomach.   If their chest rises and falls they are breathing through their chest and will find it difficult to relax.

As the person lying down breaths in deeply - relax the thumb pressure on the diaphragm area.

Ask the person lying down to slowly breath the air out of their stomach - As they do this push slowly and firmly inwards with the thumb onto the reflexology diaphragm spot.

As the person lying down takes in a new breath of air slowly release the pressure on the diaphragm spot until the thumb is simply resting on top of the diaphragm area.

Continue to repeat over and over until they are asleep. Their breathing will become more regulated, deeper and slower. You will know when to leave them by your gut instinct and practice.

This reflexology sleeping technique can take 1 - 10 minutes to help someone drift off to sleep depending on the person and their needs.

If you live on your own, then invest in a large marble that you can place under the same area of your foot whilst you're sitting watching TV about half an hour before bedtime. Simply roll the marble around the entire foot to get the biggest benefits.

If you have ticklish feet, then a simple reflexology point exists on your hands also. The pineal reflex point sits in the middle of the swirl on the soft pad of your thumb (opposite side to your nail). Apply pressure to this point and rotate for 2 - 5 mins. Do this a number of times a night to kick start the brains natural excitement that sleep is imminent.

---

*"Be the kind of person that when your feet hit the floor in the morning the devil cries 'Oh Crap! he/she is up!'"* - Anon

# Chapter Eight - The Emotional Self

Now that you have a better understanding of your brain, your mind, your body and how interlinked they are, this next chapter will highlight to you how your past illnesses may have all been within your control. Get ready to be honest with yourself.

**Your homework:**

Grab a pen and paper and list down any major illnesses that have afflicted you over your lifetime. To make things easier, start one decade ago and work forwards to today.

Then spend 10 minutes on each illness, identifying the following about each:

Where were you living? Were you happy in that house? Did you have to travel lengthy distances to get to work?

What relationship were you in at the time? Were you truly happy? Were you free to be you, or was there an underlying judgment about the things you did? Was there any resentment toward one another relating perhaps to finance or housework load? Were you in a solid relationship, or going through a break up?

What was your weight like? Were you happy with your body?

Where were you working? What was work like for you? Was it stressful, or perhaps too easy? Was it fun, or did you feel oppressed there?

What was your family unit like? Was there any fear of disappointing your parents or children?

How much fun was in your life? Was it every day or very rare?

Although there are thousands of questions I could list here, I think you're getting the idea.

If emotions and stress are linked to 90-95% of our illness, then is it possible that certain emotions and feelings are linked to EXACT locations on your body too? Louise L. Hay spent decades researching and accumulating information from her clients and groups to give us undeniable evidence that this is certainly the case. And so I took her findings further.

I looked into her claims, and I used myself as a guinea pig. I then started talking to my clients and found that Louise's work was gathering so much momentum in truth, I was excited to delve deeper.

I was not surprised when the surgeon told me I had breast cancer. I knew I had allowed the cancer to settle, and I knew why it had come. But what I didn't know at that time was why the cancer had settled in my left breast.

The answer came 2 years later after much of the research I did kept pointing back to the neural links between emotion and body.

In 2008 in Texas there was a study done with 2000 patients, all of whom could attest to a time in their lives between 18 months and 24 months before diagnosis where they had literally activated their "kill switch" by acknowledging "I can't live this way any more!" Whether it was due to a financial issue, a relationship breakdown, a work situation, or stress in general, each patient had made a determined statement that enough was enough. At that time, the mind tells the brain, "OK, this person no longer wants to live like this, so there's no point in all that hard work you're doing. Just let it all shut down".

This theory is supported in the aboriginal lore of Kadaicha, where criminals are sentenced to die by performing an ostracizing ceremony from the tribe. The Kadaicha (highest law) man points a bone at the victim and he is sent off into the outback to die. Within 3 days to 2 weeks, the victims internal systems begin to shut down and without any medical cause, they die. It is the belief behind the sentence that seems to causes the death.

Your white blood cells (lymphocytes – being the memory cells, and phagocytes – being the bad cell eaters) are told by the brain to ignore any alien cells they meet and thus the potential cancer cells in your body are left alone to fester and grow.  Your white blood cells then get used to the Cancerous cells being there, and form a memory pattern relating to those cells, effectively accepting that those cells are meant to be there, so the tumor grows and continues to grow.

But why does the Cancer form in one area of your body over another?  When the human body has millions of these pre-cancerous cells, why suddenly is one cancer cell left alone, and another is killed?

The answer lies in the work that Louise L. Hay did and the research I have since done.  I fully recommend Louise's book "You can heal your life" published by Hay House if you want to get a better understanding of her own journey.

In essence, each area of your body is linked to a different area of the brain.

18 months prior to diagnosis, I was taken away from my wonderful life in Sydney, and dragged quietly to a life in Melbourne where my partner had been offered a job of a lifetime.  I missed my friends.  I missed my routine, my runs, my job and the warmth of the ocean.  I struggled in the 40 degree heat, and freezing cold winter, so I left Melbourne 9 months later.  I picked up my 13-month-old

daughter and told my partner I'd see him back in New Zealand.

I then spent 3 months on my own, living in a house far from anyone, and I became very lonely. My partner visited on the odd weekend, and I eventually found that I was once again pregnant. Pregnancy was out of the question for me mentally, as I had specifically told my partner I had wanted only one child. So the news of a second child was one that brought only heartache and fear.

My partner did relocate back to Auckland eventually but soon was relocated once again to Wellington, meaning I spent much of my pregnancy and the birth of my 2nd child on my own. The loneliness and fear of not being able to cope alone was intense. I resented my partner for dragging me to Melbourne. I resented my partner for his days away, being able to relax and unwind without screaming toddlers and washing to be done. I resented my partner for not playing a bigger part in helping me cope.

In short, my resentment towards my partner caused my Cancer.

My Type A tendency to do everything, be everything, and never complain was the reason I developed Cancer in my Breast, specifically my left breast being that closest to the Heart. I put everyone else first and never wanted anyone to worry about me. I never once asked for help. I took this to the extreme on the night of the birth of my second child, Shelley.

I had booked myself in to a birthing clinic that was a 40 minutes drive from my house at the time. The local hospital was not a great attraction to me, so I was insistent that I would deliver my daughter in comfort. I remember that night I called my mid-wife at 1am when my contractions had reached 4-6 mins apart. My midwife calmly told me to pack my things, call my support person to collect me, and she would meet me at the birthing centre. I politely told her I'd wait a little while longer.

When I got off the phone, I called my partner in Wellington. He too advised me to call his father and get to the centre. Again, I politely declined and told him it wasn't 'so bad'!

3 hours later, I had finished cleaning the house, had vacuumed the floors and was all ready to leave the house and my toddler for a 2-night visit away. At 4 am my contractions were religiously between 3 and 4 minutes apart. Again I called my partner; but again I got off the call with only one thing running through my mind:

My support person was the elderly father of my partner. He lived 25 minutes away, and I didn't want to interrupt his sleep! I was so worried of being a nuisance, I almost had my daughter then and there on my kitchen floor!

By the time we eventually did arrive (after a very eventful trip!), my daughter could wait no more. No sooner had I walked in the door, had she popped out to say Hi.

My tendency to always put others first meant that Shelley made a dramatic entrance in to this world, which could have been entirely avoided!

Hey presto - Breast Cancer.

So here's the almighty equation of life:

**Stress dampens your immune system**

**Emotion attaches to a specific part of your body**

**When your body is not in homeostasis, inflammation and disease arise.**

> You need to reverse this chain.

Now, if ever I feel a constriction in an area of my body, I instantly review what it is that I am feeling in life. If I have lower back pain, I know I need to let go and accept my fear of financial lack. If I start coughing, I know there is something I need to say to someone.

I spent $1000 on a full check at the optometrists in 2013 after suffering from deteriorating eyesight over a period of 3 months, which resulted in the optometrist telling me that my eyes were ageing, and that I was suffering from Presbyopia (a fancy word meaning I had a loss of elasticity of the lens of my eye). I was shown the results of the test through photos he had taken of the back of my eye. Of course, the photos reaffirmed his diagnosis. His verdict? I was simply aging and there was nothing more he could do for me, other than prescribe prescription glasses. I paid the extra $1200 for the glasses, walked out and stopped using those glasses 4 days later.

"Ageing? I'm 40! I'm half way through my life! I choose not to believe what I have seen or been told". And so I sat quietly in a meeting room at my work and I asked myself "What is it that I am not willing to SEE?"

After 20 minutes and once I was sure I had the answer, I worked on releasing my perception of that situation, accepted it, and went from having difficulty seeing words on my computer screen to having 20:20 vision within the week. Those glasses are now significantly positioned next to my home computer, as a reminder never to ignore the signs from my body ever again.

As you get better at doing the actions outlined within this book, sickness and illness will become a thing of the past. You will be able to take control of any pain or ailment before it takes hold of YOU and reverse it.

*"There are 2 ways of spreading light – to be the candle or be the mirror that reflects it" – Edith Wharton*

From the years of using myself as a guinea pig and researching and investigating further, I am a firm believer in the following Brain/Body connections. These are covered in more detail in the "A to Z of DIY Health Remedies" later in this book.

## The Emotional Self

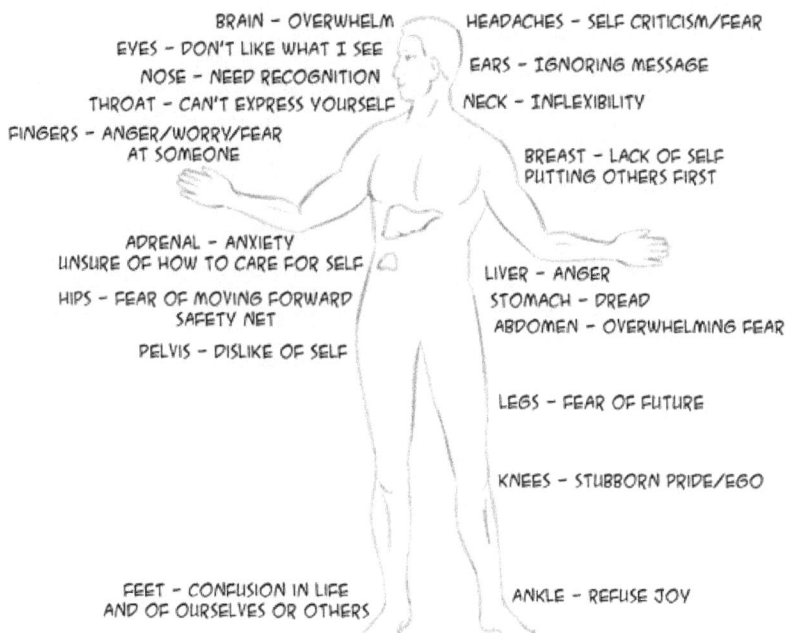

BRAIN – OVERWHELM
HEADACHES – SELF CRITICISM/FEAR
EYES – DON'T LIKE WHAT I SEE
EARS – IGNORING MESSAGE
NOSE – NEED RECOGNITION
THROAT – CAN'T EXPRESS YOURSELF
NECK – INFLEXIBILITY
FINGERS – ANGER/WORRY/FEAR AT SOMEONE
BREAST – LACK OF SELF PUTTING OTHERS FIRST
ADRENAL – ANXIETY UNSURE OF HOW TO CARE FOR SELF
LIVER – ANGER
HIPS – FEAR OF MOVING FORWARD SAFETY NET
STOMACH – DREAD
ABDOMEN – OVERWHELMING FEAR
PELVIS – DISLIKE OF SELF
LEGS – FEAR OF FUTURE
KNEES – STUBBORN PRIDE/EGO
FEET – CONFUSION IN LIFE AND OF OURSELVES OR OTHERS
ANKLE – REFUSE JOY

SPINE

UPPER BACK – UNLOVED

MID BACK – GUILT

LOWER BACK – $$ FEAR

---

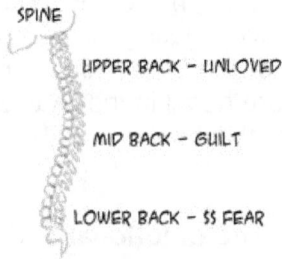

*"Mix a little foolishness with your serious plans. It is lovely to be silly at the right moment" - Horace*

# Chapter Nine - How do I balance my hormone production naturally?

## Step One - Replacement or Support

To gain some immediate sanity you can ingest some replacement hormones. Medical Doctors can prescribe some form of Hormone Replacement Therapy (HRT). **However** this is masking the underlying reason as to why you need HRT in the first place. Many of my clients are already living through HRT, believing this inevitably means their hormonal regulation is perfect. You must realise that most HRT's are focused on one hormone in particular. Leuprelin for example inhibits the production of Estrogen. It does not impact the regulation of Serotonin, or melatonin, or cortisol, or ANY other hormone in your body.

The idea that hormone replacement therapy is the be-all and end-all of hormone regulation is a myth, but only in as much as we forget to ask our doctor about the details of the drugs he or she is prescribing.

When you were a teenager you may have been given the Contraceptive Pill to stabilize often-debilitating PMS symptoms or perhaps you simply needed to regulate your periods. Sadly, the pill works by shutting down the body's natural ovarian production of hormones. Over time, your Endocrine system becomes dependent on the synthetic production of those hormones, so when it comes time to come off the pill, all hell breaks loose.

Your brain literally forgets how to regulate **natural** hormone production.

Why mess with Mother Nature when you have all the answers you need in your own body?

You can balance the regulation of your hormones by ingesting naturally forming hormones found in our every day food sources, such as:

- Warming Milk activates production of Tryptophan, a chemical that produces the Amino Acid 5HTP.  5HTP enhances production of Serotonin.

- Eating cooked Turkey meat does the same.

- Or you can buy 5HTP tablets at your local pharmacy or health shop as an immediate temporary solution.  This will help you get ONE step closer to feeling calm again.

- Eat as many phytonutrients as you can.  This means increasing your diet of leafy greens (Vegetables, that is)

## Step Two - Sleep

Make sure you get enough regenerative sleep!

I cannot shout loud enough about the benefits of regular sleeping habits, so here it is again.

- Go to bed 10 mins earlier each night, to change any late night bio-rhythm habits. Turning the light off at 10pm is optimal.

- Get up when the birds get up! Your daily production of energy hormones kicks in when the sun comes up. If you're still in bed... they aren't told to produce. Sleeping in is not helping you.

- Make sure you're kitten/puppy/partner/child is not waking you between 1am and 3am. Do everything you can to ensure you sleep through this time period.

I have included a full chapter on how to get the best out of your sleep, earlier in this book.

## Step Three - The Stress Resiliency Techniques

As your Adrenals are activated by the Nervous System, do whatever it takes to "tell" your nervous system that "everything is fine"! This means, for the mean time, you will need to "trick" your brain into believing you aren't in any danger.

You can do this in many ways:

**Conscious Breathing:** The more oxygen that reaches the blood stream, the slower your heart rate and neural activity. You USE O2 when you breathe OUT. When you breathe in the O2 latches on to the cells in your lungs, it is only released into the bloodstream during exhalation. (Next time you climb a mountain or do extreme activity where your heart rate is booming up through your throat, try to slow and extend your exhalation and see how much quicker your HR drops rather than taking larger gulps of air. It's a fun experiment).

Try this EASY technique:

- Close your eyes.
- Breathe in through your nose for a count of four (4). Concentrate only on your breath as it moves down into your diaphragm.
- Hold in for 4 counts.
- Breathe out through your mouth or nose for a count of eight (8)
- Do this six (6) times.

As you get better at this, extend your count on both inhalation and exhalation. You will be amazed that after only a short time, you will be able to slow your breath to counts of 12 or 16! The slower your breath naturally, your blood pressure drops and the less stressed you will feel.

## Change your Physiology:

- Shoulders Back!
- Chest Out.
- Chin Up
- Walk Tall.
- Plant a slight smile on your face (even if you don't feel it).
- Slow your speech.

Do these simple things and you will instantly feel better having changed your energetic vibrations immensely also.

Catch yourself out and notice any time you're feeling low what your body posture is at that moment then take action to correct it!

## Plant a fake smile on your face!

When you smile, you activate the same part of the brain that creates a real smile, which triggers endorphins and happiness. You don't have to MEAN IT, so fake it until it becomes a natural reaction.

## Change your Thought Patterns.

The symbol for "crisis" in the Chinese language is the same symbol for "opportunity". Change the way you see the world, or any situation, and you can master the art of optimising your body's natural hormone production cycles.

Changing thought patterns can be done in multiple ways. Here are two techniques that are simple and quick to master.

1.  Replace negative thoughts with different neutral or happy thoughts as soon as they come into your mind. For example, the fear of a looming court case comes into your thoughts, so instantly think about what your child needs for her lunch box the next day.

2.  Replace the intent of the negative thought, with a positive intent. Therefore, instead of focusing on your car crash being a bad event, change your perception so you focus on any positive points. To begin, you may struggle to find the positive, but as I keep stating, the more you perform these techniques the easier it becomes. Your thoughts could focus on how wonderful the tow truck driver was, how no one was hurt, and that you now get to drive around in a cool loan car for a few days!

In short, stop negative thoughts in their tracks. Less stress = more ability by your brain to balance your hormonal regulation. Yes you will still have the negative thoughts, but over time, these too will reduce in volume.

*"If opportunity doesn't knock, build a door"*

## Step Four - Eat for the health of your hormones

According to increasing amounts of research Sugar is the leading cause for estrogen increase and testosterone depletion in the human body. I use this statement as an example only to show that what you eat DOES have a direct correlation to how you feel and whether your body regulates itself for optimal health. The next section, dedicated to nutrition, will provide you with a starting point for a healthy diet, but please seek professional advice if you want to investigate this further.

## Step Five - Activate your Neural Pathways naturally through Reflexology

Reflexology is a 5000-year-old practice thought to have originated in Egypt. It is the art form of applying pressure to points on the Hands, Feet and Ears to activate neural signals and relieve blockages along neural pathways linked to other areas of the body.

You don't need to spend hundreds of dollars visiting a Reflexologist though to gain the benefits of this practice (although the relaxation component of such a visit may be enough to spur you on!).

Again, if you don't have a partner with firm thumbs who's willing to massage your feet, buy yourself a large marble and roll it around beneath your foot for 5 mins every night whilst you're watching TV.   This way you're sure to activate most of the pressure points in one hit.

To specifically activate the adrenals, find the adrenal pressure point in the arch of the foot (shown in the Appendices), and press firmly for 2-5 mins.  If you are a parent, do this for your developing teen to help them sail through puberty without the growing list of problems associated with chaotic hormonal production.

---

*"In my world, everyone's a pony and they all eat rainbows and poop butterflies!"* — *Dr. Seuss*

# Chapter Ten - Diet

I am not a nutritionist or leader in this field so I always suggest to people to choose a nutritionist or dietician who resonates with them. I have a select few that I favour as I trust their advice wholeheartedly, but one thing I am passionate about, is that your diet plays an IMPORTANT part in your overall health.

There is a reason we need food in order to survive. It is like the petrol tank on a car; if you mistakenly fill that tank with diesel when the car runs on petrol, your car will grind to a rapid halt.

Your body needs the right foods in order to be at optimal health. We spend thousands of dollars on dentists, doctors, physios, and even gym memberships without batting an eyelid. If only we had the same willingness to pay a nutritionist, our world would be a much healthier place.

It is now well publicized that the foods we eat today are not as nutrient rich as those we ate 50 years ago due to genetic modification and mass production. Large corporations want to produce more of one crop in the same sized field, thus are creating smaller, denser products without the focus being on the nutritional value of the soil.

In our parents' generation, if you knew you would be travelling long distances, you would pack a nutritional lunch in a picnic basket so you could eat along the way. These days we race out the door and hit the road, knowing we could stop at the local service station or MacDonald's if we get hungry.

Why wait until your hungry?  Why not go back to basics and ensure your house and car and office are stocked with yummy nutritional foods so that you don't need to visit the vending machine or local takeaways?  Often those easy foods are nutrient-dead and filled with additives, preservatives or sugar.

There are a few basic rules that I live by:

## Foods to avoid

If there are 3 foods that I could recommend for you to eradicate from your life, it must be these listed below where you can.

### 1.  High Fructose corn syrup

It is sugar, but of the worst kind.  It is 3x cheaper than cane sugar hence used more prolifically in mass exports such as in fizzy drinks or candy.  If you see it on a label, you know that particular food is nutrient poor and calorie rich.  When HFCS (also called Glucose-Fructose Syrup) is processed, one of the nasty bi products is mercury.  So when you drink a can of fizzy drink, you're inadvertently drinking small amounts of Mercury.

Your body uses up a lot of energy to absorb the high levels of fructose, which can cause a leaky gut, which of course leads to food allergies over time.  It also leads to a fatty liver, which leads to diabetes and liver disease.

It's not meant for human consumption.  So please, watch out for this ingredient when buying your foods.

2. **Trans fatty acid (TFA) and hydrogenated fats.**

The FDA and FSA have recently re-categorized TFA as not safe for human consumption.   It used to be a staple as an additive in processed foods to help the food stay fresh longer, have a longer shelf life and have a less greasy feel.   However, it increases your bad cholesterol levels and lowers your good cholesterol levels.

It's linked to Cancer, Type 2 Diabetes and heart disease.   It slows your digestion and creates inflammation; so why would you want it in your diet? And yet it's in most of the foods you commonly find in your pantry!

Foods to look out for that are known to use TFA:

- Commercial baked goods, such as crackers, frozen pizzas, cakes, and cookies.

- Pre-mixed cake and pancake mixes.

- Fried foods, such as doughnuts, chicken nuggets and French fries.

- Some margarines, vegetable oil and shortenings.

- Snack foods including candy, chips, and microwave popcorn

When looking out for TFA on a food label, also watch out for the words "**partially** hydrogenated" which is the marketers' way to lessen the fear associated with the acronym TFA.

### 3. **MSG (monosodium Glutamate)**

It's hidden in almost every processed food, and is found in the make up of over 50 names to make things really confusing for the average consumer. (Glutamic Acid, Vegetable Protein Extract, HVP, HPP, **Yeast Extract**, Sodium Caseinate, and Autolyzed yeast to name a few).

MSG causes over consumption of foods and uncontrollable hunger. It triples the insulin levels in the body, which causes the "spare tire" effect around your middle.

The problem in 2014 is that MANY of what we consider as healthy foods now contain some form of MSG. It's confusing. I'm confused. So I recommend just being aware and staying away from the foods that are "obvious" as a start.

It's a big bad world out there, hopefully we can survive!

## Gut Bacteria

Your gut flora plays a huge role in your overall health.

There is 3 pounds of bacteria in your gut. They regulate our food, they can cause weight gain or weight loss, and they promote our immunity. When we add sugar, we're fertilizing the bad bacteria that increase our inflammatory cells and kill the good bacteria. When the count of good bacteria reduces in your gut, the villi on the intestinal wall break down, and you are then open to leaky gut syndrome or celiac disease. Once you have a hole in your intestinal tract, any amounts of food can slip into your blood stream and activate a new allergy at any age.

It is very important to stimulate the production and health of the good bacteria in your system. So if there is one thing you can do on your journey, if nothing else, please add Probiotic yoghurt or probiotic supplements to your daily diet.

There should be one rule of thumb when planning any diet or nutritional change:

If it's from nature, then eat it. If it's man made, then don't.

Simple. God gave us all the food we needed, and we survived for thousands of years before mass production took over.

We're like cats. **Our eyes should be shining, our coats (hair) should be full and fluffy and we should have a spring in our step.** If we don't, we need to address what it is that we're eating.

## Should I go Green?

You may hear of many people who have beaten their cancer battle through choosing a radically green diet. This means juicing vegetables, drinking super-greens such as Barley Grass or Kale, and basically removing anything white from their diet.

Is this for everyone?

The medical arena will tell you to be careful with making any radical changes to your diet whilst undertaking treatment of any kind.  YOU NEED YOUR ENERGY during this time, so whilst living a cleaner existence is very important to aid your immunity, wait until after your treatment before making any such radical changes.

Why does "Going Green" seem to work?

Fruits and Vegetables contain **Phytochemicals** (or phytonutrients).  These compounds are well known to aid in the protection of healthy cells.  They regulate cancer-cell growth, modulate hormone balance, and **BLOCK carcinogen formation** or neutralize their impact on healthy cells.

Therefore, with a high amount of Phytochemicals in your body, what is a Cancer Cell to do?

They also act as powerful antioxidants to protect healthy cells and newly generated cells.

As above, I can't recommend going back to the basics of Mother Nature enough. There is growing evidence against many of the foods we eat with new studies coming out every few months. Stay ahead of the game by using your common sense.

I am in no way saying that everyone should become a vegetarian. I am however saying that we should be eating in moderation.

LESS of the bad stuff. MORE of the good stuff.

## The Miracle Super Drugs; Mother Nature at her best

There are three staples I am never found without in my cupboard. These are: Coconut Water, antioxidants and Vitamin C.

**Vitamin C** is the one Vitamin that is not formed naturally by Human Beings, Guinea Pigs or Chimpanzees. All other mammals have a natural generation of Vitamin C. When we, as humans, ingest Vitamin C, it is grabbed by the Adrenal Glands and assists in the creation of Cortisol, melatonin and serotonin. It is also currently making the rounds of the Internet as the miracle drug for healing patients of all forms of illnesses including Cancer.

**Coconut water** is not the "new" health buzz.  Its health and medicinal properties have been known for a long time.  Coconut water's chemical profile is so similar to blood plasma it has been used intravenously to save lives in developing countries and during World War II.

Research from the Philippines found drinking coconut water up to three times a week may reduce Kidney stone size and the need for surgery.

Its natural source of Cytokinins (a group of plant growth hormones) is said to assist in the regulation of human cell growth, development and anti-ageing!

It is said that if you dab a little onto your skin each day it may also reduce acne, cellulite, and eczema, stretch marks, wrinkles and age spots.

Coconut Water is high in electrolytes, zinc, selenium, iodine, manganese, ascorbic acid, and even Vitamin B, making it a good all rounder for your daily Vitamin & Mineral intake.

**Antioxidants** are the elixir of good health as far as I am concerned.  A diet high in Antioxidants has been linked to fighting and preventing cancer, and even to promote anti aging!  Antioxidants are natural protective molecules that protect the DNA in our healthy cells from damage caused by free radicals (cigarette smoke, fried food, pollution etc.)

If you think that the cost of a punnet of blueberries is the same, if not less, than one coffee, adding this treat into your daily diet just got easier!  Out of season, frozen berries can be thawed and added to probiotic yoghurt for a yummy afternoon snack or smoothie.

---

*"My doctor told me I had to stop throwing intimate dinners for four unless there are three other people." -Orson Welles*

# Chapter Eleven - Increasing your immunity

Have you ever wondered how nurses can be around sick people every day and not come home with the nastiest flu in the hospital? Are you one of those people who always seem to contract the latest bug floating around your kids' school?

Colds and Flu's are virus's. They enter into your bloodstream through the passageways in your throat or nose. These passageways, when healthy, are lined with mucous membranes that trap pathogens from entering the second layer of defense, the blood. If a virus is found in your bloodstream, your white blood cells are trained to attack! Remember how the stress response impacts the white blood cells natural killer instinct?

If your first line of defense is lowered due to poor nutrition or low PH levels in your body, you had better hope that your blood (specifically your lymphocytes), are in optimal working order! But, for the sake of this chapter, let's say they're not.

You could race to the pharmacy and order a truck load of over the counter preventative remedies OR you could ensure your body was in optimal balance to allow it to naturally defend against these viruses as they were created to do.

In my research, I have found four (4) key elements that impact immunity. These are

1. Your level of daily stress (Fight or Flight responses kick in, effectively shutting down your immunity)
2. Your PH levels (If your body's PH is too acidic, less than PH7 – 7.5, your cells stop functioning and disease and sickness occurs)
3. Balanced Hormones (See the section on hormones)
4. Balanced Diet (Remember, certain foods increase the acidity in your body, and cause added stress to your cells)

Sort these 4 aspects of your life out, and Voila, no more flu!

# Chapter Twelve – Pain Relief

Your entire body is connected through a neural pathway controlled within the brain.  The pain centre (Thalamus) sends descending signals that travel through the Medulla and spinal cord to inhibit ascending pain signals coming from the rest of your body.  All pain, or your reaction to pain, is produced within the brain, and not actually at the source.

I am forever thankful that we live in an age where we now have access to thousands of scientific research papers and evidence to support what the eastern cultures have known for thousands of years; that all pain is a reflection of what is going on in our mind.

You cannot have pain in your foot, if your brain does not know about it.

Adversely, if your brain tells you there is pain in a physical location that is no longer there (such as an amputated leg), then you will feel that pain.  (This is commonly termed Psychogenic Pain).

Every sensation you feel is analyzed by "Nociceptors" (Pain receptors), that instantly send a signal upwards to your brain.

Natural and pharmaceutical methods in pain relief are categorized depending on where in your pain pathway they act to block the transmission.

So!  The simple truth is, that if you can find a way to block the neural transmission, dull the transmission, or mimic a different transmission (thereby lying to your brain), then you have access to instant pain relief.

Of course, you could ask your doctor for

**Pharmaceutical Medications:**

Opioid Analgesics (Morphine, Demerol, Darvon, fentanyl, codeine) - Drugs that inhibit the message being sent upwards to the brain, thereby not allowing the brain to receive its message

Non-Opioid Analgesics (Aspirin, Tylenol, ibuprofen, Advil) - Drugs that act locally at the site of the pain.  The damaged tissue releases enzymes that stimulate the nociceptors.  These drugs interfere with those enzymes and reduce inflammation.

Adjuvant Analgesics (novocaine, benzocaine) - Drugs that interfere with neural transmission of the central nervous system itself.

## DIY Pain Relief options

Your first immediate step is to **ELIMINATE** all inflammatory foods in your diet!

1. Sugar - Aids inflammation by tilting your alkaline/acidity levels in your body, causing a monumental shift in your ability to reduce inflammation, and dulls your immunity.

2. White Breads / Pasta's - As above, white bread is quickly broken down in your body to glucose (sugar)

3. Animal Fats - Such as BUTTER, mince, that cheeseburger, high fatty steaks, sausages. High in saturated fat, which can lead to obesity also and increase the stickiness of your arteries.

4. Alcohol - in excess - due to most alcohol being high in sugar (as above)

5. High Fat Milk - Milk in moderation of any kind is good. However if you have 3 Latte's a day, ensure you switch to Almond Milk (which by the way has 4x the amount of Calcium than Cows Milk). Cows milk is high in Saturated Fat. Just make sure it's organic Almond Milk that doesn't contain Carrageenan (thickener)

6. MSG - Choose wisely when you're next dining out. Although there are no scientific studies conclusively linking MSA (Monosodium Glutamate) to inflammation, it is not a naturally formed product (used as a flavour enhancer in some Asian restaurants) and as such should be avoided as much as possible.

7. Trans Fats - raise LDL "bad" cholesterol and increase the risk of heart disease. But unlike saturated fats, Trans fats lower HDL "good" cholesterol and may do more damage.

The next step is to **INCREASE** the uptake of ANTI Inflammatory foods in your diet.

Some of the more common anti-inflammatory foods are:

1. **Capsaicin** - found in the Capsicum, has clinically proven to decrease arthritic pain in patients within 2 weeks of daily ingestion

2. **Salmon** - Filled with Omega 3's, has the same effect as Capsaicin

3. **5HTP** - Found in all health stores. Not only is this tablet the miracle to aid sleepless mums in the creation of Serotonin, BUT it has also been shown to reduce the onset and intensity of headaches! Note: Warm cows milk, or cooked turkey meat has the same effect.

4. **Coffee** - assists by reducing the blood flow and neural impulses that promote the pain receptors in the brain

5. **Ginger** - Other than the well known effects of reducing nausea, Ginger is an excellent herb for migraines and heartburn, and is a wonder cure for Menstrual Pain!!

6. **Rosemary** - This herb naturally eases nerve and muscle tension. Rosemary has also been clinically proven to reduce chronic headache pain, and assists in promoting the anti-aging process of skin damage.

7. **Chamomile** - An anti-inflammatory agent that helps almost everywhere in the body! It is also a very calming herb, which helps you to relax, thereby having a further effect of reducing your body's natural production of inflammatory hormones.

8. **Turmeric** - The "wise" one.  Turmeric is well known as a natural antiseptic and antibacterial agent.  One of its components, curcumin eases inflammatory conditions such as psoriasis and rheumatoid arthritis.  Sprinkle turmeric on your food to add the impact but lessen the amount if this taste is not for you.  Great for treating cuts and burns, and is well known as an anti-aging spice due to its cleansing properties of your blood.  (Anti-dementia agent)

9. **Sage** - A herb from the mint family, Sage reduces pain in muscles and has been known to assist in removing blocks in the brain (clear thinking - aromatic)

10. **Fenugreek** - Not naturally found in our usual western diets, this herb is beginning to become one of our super-foods for its anti-inflammatory properties AND its ability to reduce high triglyceride blood levels, reducing your chances of heart disease

11. **Echinacea** - one more reason to add Echinacea to your diet, thanks to its cooling properties to a sore throat

12. **Oranges** - While Vit C has been linked to helping cure the common cold and even in some cases curing Cancer, Oranges also contain an antioxidant called beta-cryptoxanthin which helps

reduce the risk of anti-inflammatory conditions such as rheumatoid Arthritis. (The same antioxidant is also found in veggies such as the NZ Kumara, sweet potato and cantaloupe)

13. **Flaxseed & Linseed** - Very high in Omega 3. Well known for their anti-inflammatory properties as well as analgesic. Commonly found in food stores as LSA (Linseed, Sunflower, Almond) - Sprinkle over your morning muesli or add to smoothies for a change in texture.

14. Replace your Vegetable Oils for healthy oils such as Olive or Coconut when cooking.

# Other Non Dietary Pain relieving options

## Ice

Ice helps by acting as a local anesthetic and by slowing the nerve impulses which in turn interrupts the pain-spasm reactions between nerves in the affected area

## CQ

Recently on the market in most chemists, CQ (Cissus quadrangularis) promotes bone health and reduces pain. CQ is currently being endorsed to athletes to reduce the effects of constant impact during high intensity sports.

### Reflexology

See the Reflexology appendices at the end of this book for more information on DIY pressure points to relieve pain. 2-5 mins of pressure on these points should be enough to offer you instant pain reduction.

### Do something FUN

This is THE most important and easiest DIY Pain relief mechanism - Find some way to enjoy a 10 minute BELLY-ACHING laugh and you will open a window for yourself of TWO hours of pain relief. **Laughter** has been proven to be as effective and in some cases, MORE effective than medical drugs to relieve pain. Google "Norman Cousins", the author who laughed himself back to health after being diagnosed with a life threatening form of arthritis.

### Take your mind away

When you know something is about to happen, such as an injection, your perception of the event will cause your pain receptors in the brain to go into overdrive. If you DON'T see the event happening, the pain is much less. If the nurse doesn't tell you that she is about to inject you, yes you feel a twinge of pain, but nothing close to the pain you WOULD have felt had you watched the whole affair.

It is also well known that pain is far worse when it is happening TO us, rather than BY us. If you were to tickle your own hand, the ticklishness is far less than if someone else were to tickle you.

So it really does work to focus your mind on other things. Count backward from 100 out loud. This takes the focus off the pain at hand. Go inward and plan a trip in your mind. Concentrate on your breathing - see it flow in through your nose and down into your diaphragm. Watch it as it flows back up through your throat and out through your mouth again. When you concentrate on your breath (your nasal passages are connected to your brain), you can't focus on anything else.

## Contra the pain site

Why is it that we're told to rub the opposite Big toe when we stub our toe as a child?

Have you ever tried to rub your left knee when you bang your right knee into a table?

This is called "Competitive Inhibition". You are effectively sending your brain a competing pain signal, so your brain has to distinguish which pain it should "tell" you about!

So next time you bang into something, reach down and DON'T rub the pain point, rub briskly and quite hard, the OPPOSITE side of your body!

It has been proven that even THINKING about the opposing site and intensifying your focus there, reduces the actual pain felt from the original pain point.

# The DIY Bible

## *The WOF Challenge*

Ready to eradicate Stress from your life?

Whilst moving through your adventures in Stress relief, to find what works for you, there is one pathway I know works for 90% of my clients. Why does it not work for the other 10%? Well, most of this process is about resetting your brain and removing any desire for control. You can't make someone believe in themselves if they're not open to trying. And thus I don't – try, that is. In order to start on the healing journey in the next section it is mandatory to have mastered the following challenge steps first. Don't beat yourself up if you don't 'get it' first time. It took me years to truly understand the level of commitment needed to find deep happiness.

The answer to fully eradicating stress from your life forever is to find yourself again; to love yourself. When you have truly let go of your ego, other people's opinions no longer take hold and you feel lighter and more at peace. You will be untouchable, inspired, inspiring, and most of all; loved.

When love replaces judgment in everything you do, there will be no more room for anguish, or hate, or worry. Your pathway to leading a happy life becomes clearer. The fastest way to find yourself is to ask "How am I expanding?"

We all have a need to continuously evolve. When we stop expanding, we stagnate. When we stagnate, we feel less than ourselves; we feel oppressed and frustrated and expand our feelings of resentment. Look for ways to expand within your life, such as learning something new, meeting new people, seeking new experiences – and you would have fulfilled the first of many essential human needs.

The steps outlined in the WOF Challenge will, I know, set you on a course of discovery. I wish you well on your journey. Make sure you keep me posted with your progress on my blog! I'd love to hear from you.

## Step One: Conscious Breathing.

Breathe in through your nose **slowly**, ensuring you fill your lungs. Gently release and exhale.

Concentrate only on your breath. Feel it, imagine its pathway in through your nostrils and down to your lungs. When you concentrate on your breath, your mind switches away from all other thought. This is your time to really 'Stop'.

If you're finding it hard to concentrate on your breath, close your right nostril to ensure you inhale only through the left nostril. This activates the right hemisphere of the brain, which is your calming side. Your left brain (think, think, think!) is forced to stop working and take a short break.

The slower and deeper you breathe, the better. Practice daily. Soon you will notice that whenever you feel stress coming on you can instantly reduce your reactive thoughts by performing this simple exercise.

How long do you breathe for? Whatever feels necessary to you. I practice conscious breathing every morning before I rise from bed, and at least twice during the day. This should become a routine for you to activate daily. Remember, you are gifting your brain with much needed oxygen. Make this moment count.

## Step Two: Become the Witness

*Challenge 1*

Commit to practicing this task for 10 minutes each day for the first week.

During the next week, commit to an hour.

The week after, see if you can go an entire morning.

Continue expanding the timeframe for this task until it becomes natural and effortless. This is truly life changing if you allow yourself to fully indulge.

Start today. Go for a 10-minute walk. As you walk, slow your gait. Keep your head raised. Make eye contact with as many people as you can. Don't look down. Be present and committed to be aware of your surroundings. Take an intensive review of what colours you see. Notice the people around you - does that person look happy or sad? What are they wearing? Most importantly, when you look at each person, notice him or her, but do NOT think about them and don't linger long.  You will find yourself quietly saying things like "she really shouldn't wear that colour", "he needs a haircut", or "she's overweight".

You may laugh now, but even the most loving individuals have these quiet thoughts without actually realizing it!  Remember that 90% of your thoughts are from your subconscious.  You can't help those thoughts from appearing.  At least, you can't YET.

Once you start to take notice (and I mean FULLY notice) your surroundings and the thoughts you hear in your head with conscious attention, you will be astounded at how many negative thoughts you really do have within this short time.   How can you strive to be a happy person if you are unaware of the thousands of habitual negative thoughts that hammer your brain on a daily basis?  You're fighting with only 10% of your mighty power, trying to win against the 90% force of your subconscious.  The odds just don't stack up.  The only way to win is to take control of those subconscious thoughts and retrain them.

So how do you stop these judgmental thoughts from appearing?  At first, you don't – simply being aware allows for the first shift to take place.  When you notice a negative thought, start replacing it with a NICE thought.  So, if you thought someone should really go on a diet due to his or her size, think "what a lovely colour she's wearing today".  Get it?

Believe me, this step is the hard one!  Challenge yourself.  And see what comes up for you.  Don't beat yourself up for those recurring thoughts, just allow them to be, and start replacing them slowly.

Once you master becoming less involved and more of a silent witness only, your thoughts become clearer and you'll have a better command over those that are intrusive.  You will become more present and notice things in your environment that perhaps had gone unnoticed by you for years.

### Challenge 2:

Try this at work.  Walk into a meeting and just quietly observe those around you instead of actively participating in their quarrel or complaint.  Witness and replace all your judgments and thoughts where you find them with nice statements about those people.  Just your shift in awareness will change the energy in that room.  You may even find that people stop complaining in your company, and that all your meetings from that point forward go smoothly and effortlessly.

## Step Three:  The Gratitude Game

Ah!  So you've heard this mumbo jumbo about being grateful before, but really struggle with finding anything to be happy about? Well, here's the prelude. You've just successfully found things to be happy about in Step Two. When you are forced to replace judgment with loving thoughts about others, the same thought patterns become easier in your own life.

You don't need to be grateful about big events or people. You could start with things like the following:

- I love the colour yellow
- I love how freshly washed sheets feel when I climb into bed at night
- My cat brings me unconditional love when I need it
- I am so lucky to have a roof that doesn't leak!
- Thank goodness for electricity
- I absolutely love Lasagna.

So before you go to bed tonight, you don't need to write a gratitude journal, but you do need to sit quietly in your bedroom and think of five (5) things you are happy or grateful about.

That's all!

If you start this journey in a real funk, and are truly struggling with this challenge, try this simple technique that works like a charm.

## Gratitude Technique:

Find a comfortable seated position and close your eyes. Start by consciously breathing until your mind and body are both relaxed. Then move through the following senses, taking only 1 minute on each.

So, begin by bringing to the front of your mind a memory or **SIGHT** that instantly brings a smile to your face. It could be your Child's face, or a holiday you once had, or a group of friends laughing, or perhaps a time when you were the focus of accolades at work. Whatever it is, bring it to your minds eye, and imagine it as if it were real and happening to you right now. **Feel the emotions**. See the colours. Hear the laughter. Be present and fully involved. You WANT to feel that emotion again. You want the feeling of happiness to envelope you now.

After a few moments, gently let that memory or picture fade and replace it with a **SMELL** that reminds you of a time when you were happy. It could be a cologne, or flower, or freshly cut grass, or coffee brewing. Whatever it is, bring it to your minds eye and imagine it as if it were present right now. Smell it. Feel it. Let the emotions of the presence of that smell waft through you and relax you now.

After a few moments more, gently let the smell fade away, and replace it with a **SOUND** that evokes a sense of love or peace. Is it a bird call, a child's laughter, a song, cicadas chirping?  Whatever it is, bring it to your minds eye right now, as if it were being played loud and clear.  Listen.  Hear it.  Feel the emotions it brings.  Smile, and let it take you away.  Feel love for that sound.

After a few moments, gently let the sound fade away, and replace it now with a **TASTE** that instantly makes you feel at peace or filled with pure joy.  Is it your favourite food, or a taste from your childhood?  Is it a freshly made scone or cup of coffee?  Perhaps it's a glass of wine at the end of a hard day.  Whatever your taste is, imagine you have it there in front of you now, take a sip or a big bite, and taste it.  Let your mouth literally taste that item as if it were real.  Witness how it makes you feel.  Let the emotion engulf you and fill you with joy.  Sit in this moment and enjoy.  Breathe.

And now let it go.  Finally, find a sense of TOUCH that you love.  Examples could be the feeling of running water in a forest stream, or running your fingers through your partners' hair, hands on silk, hands through soft fur or feeling wind on your face.  Imagine the feeling of touching your favourite item.  It is real.  It is now.  Let that feeling warm your heart and bring a smile to your face.  Feel at peace.  Breathe, and then slowly, gently let it go.

Now that you are in the "zone" of gratitude, go back and try to come up with those 5 things that you can be grateful for.

The more you do this, the more things you will notice during the day that you start lodging away for this exercise at night!

**Handy tip**: If your kids are driving you insane fighting in the back seat of your car, teach them the Grateful Game. The moment they start fighting again, ask them to take turns shouting out what 5 things they are happy for that day. Depending on the age of your kids, they can come up with some real pearlers! My 3-year-old daughter brought a smile to my face when she declared that she was happy for the colour yellow because it made mummy happy! Wonderful.

This game changes the energy in the car instantly and allows for a happier journey to or from the schoolyard!

## Step Four: Lift your energy

Make it your mission to increase your energy field. We all have one. Remember that your entire body is one large vessel of electrical pulses and energy and it radiates beyond the confines of your physical body. You've heard people talk about seeing Aura's. Well, they definitely exist whether you can see them or not – an aura is energy represented as light.

Have you ever wondered about the impact some people have on you when they enter your personal space? Perhaps they moved towards you too quickly, or stood too close when being introduced. I am impacted very quickly by someone's presence in my zone, and as a New Zealander we're lucky to have been brought up in an environment where our personal space is larger than most other countries.

What is it you're feeling, as you subtly shift your feet to distance yourself slightly? Their energy field has imposed on yours, leaving you instantly exposed and vulnerable. Some have described this feeling as pushing them out of their "comfort zone". This experience can leave you feeling at odds, sparking your brain to think up ways to hastily make an exit!

We all have a personal space. Whether yours is large or small will determine whether perhaps you are that person who is the imposer, or the retreater. Becoming aware of your own personal space boundaries, and therefore the limit of your physical energy field (as there are many other energy layers beyond that), allows you to both protect yourself from feeling 'attacked' whilst also ensuring you are respectful of how you impact others.

When you feel low, your energy field becomes retracted. People are no longer *attracted to* you. You feel it, whether you have noticed it or not. It happens more than we think – picture a time recently when you've walked into a room and felt a sense of dread; of suffocation; of lethargy; or even had a real sense of negativity come over you. What you're feeling is the energetic vibration of someone else in that room. Negative energy is powerful, and unless you block it, it can impact your own energy and emotions very quickly.

Perhaps you work in an office where the people around you use complaints as a regular mode of starting a conversation. Perhaps you've noticed that you always feel tired after you've been to a friend's house or to a particular shop or mall in your area. Unless you're someone who is aware of the energy in a room, you've probably never actually noticed the connection to your feelings after the encounter.

Remove the frequency of being in environments that are energetically depleting and PRESTO, your energy levels go up and things instantly start to feel so much easier in your life. One simple change can make a very big difference to your overall health and wellbeing.

Whereas, have you ever noticed that person at work who seems larger than life? They're always happy and move with intent, and for some reason people gravitate toward that person? Jealous? You have the power to be that person. All you need to do is lift your own energetic vibration even if a natural introvert.

If you are stuck at home alone on a daily basis, get out and about and be regenerated through the energy of others - whether this is simply by being at a café, walking on a crowded beach or doing a Yoga or Zumba class - anything helps. Where there are people, there is energy that you can feed off. Make it your mission to meet as many new people in your work place as you can in one week. See where that gets you!

And change your body language!  Remember to pull those shoulders back, chin is up, eyes focused ahead, walk tall and with purpose.  The moment you slouch your shoulders and drop your head, your energy field lowers.  Keep it bold.  Keep it large.  Keep it open.  And whenever you can, simply bring a slight smile to your mouth.  Fake it, until it becomes a natural disposition!

I'd like to warn you away from spending too much time in malls though.  Although the energy amongst crowds is usually helpful, malls seem to breed a negative energy.  People aren't relaxed when they're pulling husbands and children from shop to shop, thus I find that malls can reduce your energy field and bring you lower than prior to your visit.

To raise your energy levels instantly, Google search any of the basic Qi Gong exercises which take only 2-5 minutes to do, and can be done anywhere.

## Step Five:  Seek, and you shall find...FUN

You are an amazing creature.  Your body, brain and mind are OUT OF THIS WORLD!  So why are you not enjoying every moment of your life?  Make a stand and commit, RIGHT NOW to infusing more laughter and fun into your daily life.

Yes, but how!?

(That's easy.)

Although you may be lacking in the very hormones that cause us to feel happy and loved, there is a way to re-spark those hormones into production. Laugh, laugh and laugh some more!

Think. What used to make you laugh? Did you enjoy stand up comedy, or funny movies, or the Super Bowl ads, a tickle session, or social interactions with friends? Whatever you used to enjoy that made you laugh A LOT, seek out again.

I find that downloading some funny YouTube videos off the Internet is a great start (like the Funniest Super Bowl ads). Watch or listen to these on your way to work in the mornings. The best way to start any day is with laughter and a smile on your face. Start the day well, and the rest of the day invariably follows suit.

If you're still struggling to know where to find laughter, seek out Laughter Clubs in your area, or Laughter Yoga; schedule a fun evening with your friends regularly. Or simply sign up to receive a daily joke in your inbox.

The more you laugh, the easier it will be to find fun, and to lose that stress.

## Step Six: The 7 hour Sleep

You now know the importance of sleep. Without it your body cannot heal. Without deep regenerative sleep, your hormones will not replenish. You will wake up in the morning feeling tired, and your ability to stay calm when under pressure will be at an all time low. Sleep is THE most important step in the WOF Challenge. Without it, you reduce your life span, and you'll struggle with any of the steps above.

So, your mission is to find 7 hours of DEEP UNINTERRUPTED sleep every night.

Buy earplugs if you need to!

The rules are simple. Remove all technology from your bedroom. Turn off bright lights and TV within 30 minutes prior to retiring to bed.

Lights off by 10:30pm (no excuses). Waking up by 6:30am at the latest.

Eradicate the probability of being woken between 1am and 3am (hence the ear plugs).

After only 4 days your body will begin to fall into its natural biorhythms once more, which will set you back on track for regaining your sanity.

Remember - don't sleep in. If you are tempted to have a nap during the day, do this in the afternoon between 1 and 3pm only so as not to impact your natural energy cycles.

And there you have it, 'The 6 Step WOF Challenge to easy Stress Relief'.

Sleep

Become a Witness

Breathe

The WOF Challenge

Laugh

The Grateful Game

Sounds easy?  Well, it's not a one-time gig.

The challenge is for you to embed this into your daily life until it becomes a habit.  More breathing, less involvement, higher energy fields, better sleep, more gratitude and more laughter – daily, constantly and slowly, without addressing any other area of your life, you will see a huge shift in the way you perceive otherwise stressful moments, and you'll feel happier, healthier and emotionally stronger.

*"If you let yourself be blown to and fro, you lose touch with your root.  To be restless is to lose one's self-mastery"*

*Lau-tzu (Tao Te Ching)*

# The DIY Health Hug

So are you ready to start your healing process?

If you can honestly say that you know you have the ability to heal yourself, all you needed was this belief to make it so. I believe in you, and I can say this because I've witnessed this happen time and time again. I've witnessed healing outside of modern medicine and I know this to be true; You DO have the power to heal. Believe it. And it is so.

Take charge of your mind and give it permission to do what it does best - Keep you alive.

One caveat on the following process though is that you first complete, successfully, the WOF Challenge in the previous chapter, which teaches you some of the practices needed for this healing. **Please do not just jump into this**, as your results may be less than optimal without first building your foundation practice.

I suggest reading through this chapter a few times first, so you come to understand the process fully, and the reasoning behind each step.

To get the best results from this practice, find a quiet room somewhere where you know you will not be disturbed for 60 minutes. Turn down the lights to a soft glow, allowing you to further relax.

## Step One: Awaken your mind

Start this Health Hug process by increasing neural activity to the brain; with a clear message relating to the area you wish to heal. You can do this easily through simple reflexology on the foot, the ear or the hand.

For example, if you have Breast Cancer, you would firmly press the point on your foot or hand that relates to the Breast. Do so for 5 minutes. Then gently move onto the next step in this process. A set of full reflexology charts is located in the appendix.

Else, simply focus all thoughts on the area fully and breathe…

## Step Two:  Reflect

You should know that your illness or pain was probably caused by some emotional stress in your life, unless you were impacted by environmental triggers or fell victim to accidental or malicious attack. With this in mind, you will need to locate the experience or emotional stressor from your memory that propelled you to this state of being. You can do this through visiting a practitioner who can help you OR you can do this yourself, as described below.

Close your eyes and take a few deep breaths in through your nose, whilst gently relaxing and reducing the noise in your head by solely focusing only on your breath. Once you feel a certain peace (after 2-3 minutes), and you can breathe gently without the noise of the world coming in to your head, simply ask yourself over and over again "Why have I caused this pain?" (Or illness / disease / affliction / Allergy, whatever etc)

Over a period of minutes, if you just rest in the question, the answer will show up for you. **Trust** in the first answer. Don't worry if you think you planted it there. Usually you already know what is true.

Once you have your answer, go back to the section on the Emotional Self (or go forward to Section Five) to reflect and check in. Does this resonate with you? If the answer is yes, proceed to step 3. If the answer feels forced, or unlikely (usually due to outside noise or interruptions), stop this process for the evening and begin again another time.

## Step Three:  Respond

Well done.  You've already started your journey into healing.  Acknowledging that you have caused your own illness, and giving the cause a name has propelled you forward in reaching your desired destination.

Allow yourself to recall the memory and feelings that surrounded the point in time that sparked your illness. Witness it, but don't judge it.  Don't think to yourself, "I hate that" or "I should never have…"  Simply watch the memory as if you were an innocent bystander. And breathe.

At the end of your memory, say to yourself, "I lovingly let you go now" or "I am safe and happy now".

I have found 3 powerful tools to help in this step. It is your choice which tool you choose to adapt here.

1. Witness the memory, breathe (as above), state your intention (as above) – then breathe again, and start the memory from the beginning. Relive it over and over and over again. Each time, breathe, witness, and state your intention. With each memory recall, you are reducing your brain's memory of the emotional hurt. You are telling your brain that everything worked out ok. There is no longer any need to feel under attack from this memory. It is often helpful to rope a friend in to talk you through this gentle process.

2. As you focus on the memory, begin gently tapping (EFT, Emotional Freedom Tapping). I won't delve into this practice in too much detail here, so please Google this term to find out more. For this exercise, EFT is simple in that you are tapping meridian pressure points that are located around your face and upper body. Begin by karate chopping the side of your palm (just down from your little finger), then move along the meridian points every 5-10 seconds, using 2 fingers. The next point is just inside your eyebrows (where they almost meet); then to the

outer point of both eyes; then directly under your eyes (mid point); then under the outer corner of both nostrils; then in the crease of your chin below your mouth; then in the soft spot below your clavicle bone; then under your arms (at the bra line, so a few cm's below your armpit); and lastly to the crown of your head. (A picture of these points is located in the Appendix). Tap as you witness the memory, and keep telling yourself that you are now safe and that you lovingly let go of any hurt or anger caused by this memory. "I am safe, and I love myself unconditionally" "I am fully healed now". Some people only need to do a few rounds of EFT to make a difference. How many rounds you do is completely up to you. Often it may be necessary to repeat this step over 3 to 5 days (10 mins at a time)

3. Instead of focusing on a memory, you can focus in on the FEELING and begin asking yourself whether that feeling is true. What do I mean by this? An example always helps. If you find yourself focused on the arthritis that has started to encroach through your fingers, you may have identified in the previous step that there was an area of your life that you are less than happy about and feel resentment for that situation. So here you stop and really analyze that feeling. If you were to see that situation in a positive light, how could you view it? For example, you're resentful that your husband/wife always spends the weekly budget before it hits the bank account. Reframe that thought. There are

multiple ways you could see this differently, you just need to find the one that resonates and fits with you successfully. Perhaps you could see your partner for the loving person they are, and realise they spend that money on the family because they love doting on others. If you sit in silence, for as long as it takes, and analyze your feeling and your thoughts behind those feelings to find a positive way to view that situation or event, the power of your emotions will reduce significantly. Continue to do this exercise for as long as it takes for you to release that emotion and truly feel that you have accepted what WAS and have let it go.

Just a personal note here; this was the exact technique I used myself to heal from the onset of arthritic fingers. I started in a position of resentment and frustration and ended feeling so much lighter and more in love with the target of my initial resentment. Score!

Again, it is your choice which of these options you choose to perform. Or you can try all of them for good effect!

This is a very difficult step, hence my recommendation to complete the WOF Challenge first in order to get you 'ready' for this task. Once you have identified the reason for your illness or pain, then FULLY released the emotion that caused it, your pain will dissipate. It might slowly reduce over a number of days, or you may find it almost instantly abates.

# Step Four: Healing Meditation

I suggest performing a healing meditation every evening before you go to bed for a number of weeks. Not only does it work miracles, it also sets you up for a wonderful deep sleep!

To make things simple you can download this meditation from my website or record your own voice on your Dictaphone or iPhone for instant playback. This meditation should take between 15-20 minutes only.

Sit or lie down (as long as you are not prone to falling asleep when fully relaxed). Find a comfortable position. I prefer my legs crossed like a child, on a cushion on the floor. I suggest sitting with your back against a wall for your first few times to support your core.

If you've already completed the WOF Challenge you would have already performed the first half of this meditation (the Gratitude Meditation), so briefly read through and continue reading from the "Additional Step" for further instructions.

**Meditation:**

Close your eyes.

Begin by focusing on your breath. Breathe in and witness your breath coming in through your nose, down your throat and into your lungs and heart region.

Witness (visualize) your breath then following the same track back up and out as you exhale (either through your nose or mouth).  To make things easier for you, some people prefer to count as they inhale.  Count in for 4 seconds, hold for 2 seconds, and exhale for 6 seconds.

With each breath, consciously relax your body.  Start with your forehead, then your cheek muscles, your jaw, relax your throat, your shoulders, your back.  Relax your fingers, your hands, your arms.  Relax your toes, your feet, your leg muscles, and your butt.

Take your time just breathing and relaxing.  When you feel you are ready, you will begin visualising sensory objects in order to lift your energetic vibration, and to expand the love in your heart before moving into the healing focus.

So, begin by bringing to the front of your mind a memory or **SIGHT** that instantly brings a smile to your face.  It could be your Child's face, or a holiday you once had, or a group of friends laughing, or perhaps a time when you were the focus of accolades at work.  Whatever it is, bring it to your minds eye, and imagine it as if it were real and happening to you right now.  **Feel the emotions**.  See the colours.  Hear the laughter.  Be present and fully involved.  You WANT to feel that emotion again.  You want the feeling of happiness to envelope you now.

After a few moments, gently let that memory or picture fade and replace it with a **SMELL** that reminds you of a time when you were happy.  It could be a cologne, or flower, or freshly cut grass, or coffee brewing. Whatever it is, bring it to your minds eye and imagine it as if it were present right now. Smell it. Feel it. Let the emotions of the presence of that smell waft through you and relax you now.

After a few moments more, gently let the smell fade away, and replace it with a **SOUND** that evokes a sense of love or peace. Is it a birdcall, a child's laughter, a song, cicadas chirping? Whatever it is, bring it to your minds eye right now, as if it were being played loud and clear. Listen. Hear it. Feel the emotions it brings. Smile, and let it take you away. Feel love for that sound.

After a few moments, gently let the sound fade away, and replace it now with a **TASTE** that instantly makes you feel at peace or filled with pure joy. Is it your favourite food, or a taste from your childhood? Is it a freshly made scone or cup of coffee? Perhaps it's a glass of wine at the end of a hard day. Whatever your taste is, imagine you have it there in front of you now, take a sip or a big bite, and taste it. Let your mouth literally taste that item as if it were real. Witness how it makes you feel. Let the emotion engulf you and fill you with joy. Sit in this moment and enjoy. Breathe.

And now let it go. Finally, find a sense of TOUCH that you love. Examples could be the feeling of running water in a forest stream, or running your fingers through your partners' hair, hands on silk, hands through soft fur or feeling wind on your face. Imagine the feeling of touching your favourite item. It is real. It is now. Let that feeling warm your heart and bring a smile to your face. Feel at peace. Breathe, then slowly, gently let it go.

## Additional Step:

Now that you have successfully invited love and joy into your heart and lifted your energy vibration, bring your focus to your third eye, which is the space between your two eyes, whilst keeping your eyes closed.

Witness a small glowing white light forming just in front or above your third eye / forehead. As you breathe, notice the white light getting more intense. Slowly let the white light grow and begin its journey into your brain, down your throat, to find its path to your heart where it stays a while.

With each breath, notice how the white light circulates your heart and gets bigger and bigger and bigger. Feel the energy force from the light. Feel the heat in your heart. Take a few moments and let this white light settle in the joy and love in your heart. Smile upon it. Feel its desire to heal you. Believe in its energy. (This is the important bit!)

Now intentionally visualize the movement of this white ball of energy down or upward towards your pain point, affliction or disease. Notice the colour of the disease or ailment. Is it black, or red, or brown? Perhaps it's blue, no matter, just notice its colour. Move the white light to this area, and witness it slowly wipe away the pain, the disease, and the colour with its movements. Let the white ball expand over this area slowly (and if it is your entire body, then let it expand and grow to fully encompass you entirely).

Spend a few minutes just breathing, and letting this white glowing ball fill this area of your body with love and healing.

When you feel satisfied, gently allow and witness the white light to move back along its original path, back up to your minds eye (that point between your eyebrows). Once there, silently give it gratitude for taking away the pain, then watch as the light moves outside of your body. Then push it away. Push it with all your might and heart. Watch as it fades into the distance.


Breathe and stay in the silence of this moment.


And when you are ready, slowly bring your focus back to your physical body by gently wiggling your fingers and toes, and open your eyes.

And know you have just started your healing process.

Do not doubt it.

Do not give your ailment, disease or pain any further thought today.

Repeat this each night until you feel fit and healthy once more.

# Step Five:  Post operative Care

So you made it through the hard stuff!  It's easy sailing from here on in, but to seal your commitment to your healing process, follow through with these few simple rules.

1. Start planning a big event or trip within the next 3 months.  Don't wait for next year.  Don't plan it for 6 months time.  You need something to really, really look forward to within the next 90 days.  Do it for me.  Do it for yourself.  And make it a fun experience without added stress!

2. Increase your fun and happiness quotient any way you can!  You must seek out fun.  It won't come to you.  Make it happen.  Be your social network event organizer!  Put a calendar on your fridge and note down at least one social or fun outing EVERY week.  Don't think of this as a chore, think of this as your survival checklist!

3. Remember – Laugh DAILY

4. Eat to sustain your body and mind.  This means eating for nutrition and planning ahead!  Add more greens in the mornings and your sugar cravings will go away.

5. Continue your healing meditation for 2 weeks. You probably won't need to, but what's the harm, right!? It also gives you the excuse to stop thinking those 4,000 thoughts that race through your head each hour.

And that's got to be good for you!

Awaken
your Mind

Post
Operative
Care

DIY
Health
Hug

Reflect

Meditate

Respond

*"You need not fear the darkness when the light is everywhere" – Lao-tzu*

# The A to Z of DIY Health Remedies

Tired of spending hundreds of dollars every month on over the counter prescriptions or therapies? Many of our toughest ailments can actually be fixed by Mother Nature or by our own minds, thereby saving you your retirement fund! This section is filled with nuggets that have never failed me yet.

Part natural remedies, part emotional healing, this section has been compiled from 4 years of investigation, scientific research, personal experience through healing others, and using myself as a guinea pig.

The findings here lend themselves from the Emotional Self section earlier in this book also.  The following remedies are meant to be quick and accessible, for you to access only when and if you need to.  The purpose of this section is to be a reference guide for your own DIY health hug to enable you to quickly skip to the heading that describes your pain.  It is not expected that you, the reader, sits here quietly for the next 2 hours reading line for line.

The Ailments and Pain area's listed below are in alphabetical order and cover many of today's common complaints.  I hope the findings from my journey are as valuable to you as they were to me, as I live through each day pain and stress free.  My greatest wish is to eradicate the world from stress and thereby also eradicating illness from our world.  Fires start with one ember – that's all that is needed.  One person, one change at a time, and hopefully by sharing your own story, you also can start a fire of change.

Disclaimer:

Please do seek medical advice in the event of serious pain or symptoms.

# *The Common List of Ailments*

## Adrenal Fatigue

### The Low Down

AF is caused when the body feels like it is under constant attack. Your Adrenal system grows tired of continuous activation and effectively slows down.

### The Fix

Shunt your Endocrine System into overdrive again by prompting homeostasis of hormones. Please see a doctor or nutritionist to identify if you are low on DHEA before taking any pills. See the many tips and tricks within this book (reflexology / leafy greens / laughter / falling in love / meditation / EFT for examples) and re-read chapter eight.


## Ankle Pain

### The Emotional Low Down

Are you currently refusing Joy in your life?

### The Fix

You may think you're happy enough. But ask the hard question: When was the last time you TRULY laughed for any length of time. You should strive to find what makes you happy, and flood your life with such experiences. Usually Ankle pain comes along when you're feeling less than happy though, therefore you need to reflect seriously on WHY you feel this way, and deal with that situation or thought pattern as a priority.

## Abdominal Pain

### The Emotional Low Down

Overwhelming Fear – of the future, of a current predicament, or of the possibility of loss?

### The Fix

Abdominal pain is not only linked with fear, it is also linked with feeling less than self, meaning you need to ask yourself what you are worried about, what are you fearful of, what is it that you are missing out on in life, and inject the opposite situation or thought pattern into your brain.

For example if you are fearful of speaking in front of an audience but have been asked to do so in the coming weeks, you can sit quietly, and imagine the scene as if you were there already, then breathe consciously through the scene, noticing the colours and the sounds, and smile at individually recognized faces.

The more you run the scenario through your mind, from start to finish, the brain will acclimatize and reduce its fear as it begins to recognize the situation as a normal occurrence. Generally what we fear is the fear of what we DON'T KNOW. Replace any fear with a possible GOOD scenario and your fear will evaporate. (Or start with EFT if you need more help)

This works exceptionally well with children who show symptoms of lower tummy ache a week or so before a big event.

# Acid Reflux

## The Emotional Low Down

Dread – Linked also to the Stomach

## The Immediate Fixes

If you often get a burning sensation in your stomach, chest or throat, this may be caused by stomach acids being over productive and irritating your esophagus.

To Alleviate:  Do NOT lie down after eating.  If you must, keep your upper body elevated with a cushion.

Stop smoking, as this aggravates reflux

**Avoid** the following foods, which help to relax the valve between your stomach and esophagus:

- Alcohol,
- Caffeine,
- Chocolate,
- Tomatoes,
- Onions,
- Garlic,
- Citrus fruits

Investigate options to reduce the acid forming foods in your diet.  An alkaline diet will calm the over activity and excess production of stomach acid.

## The long term fixes

Fix reflux long term by reducing your acid forming foods and upping the intake of alkaline forming foods (greens). See the FIX section of Abdominal Pain to see a breakdown on how to reduce your dread.


# Anxiety

### The Low Down

Anxiety presents itself either when you've suffered through periods of chronic stress (thus effectively your hormones are so out of whack that you're depleted of any calming neurochemicals) OR something in your environment has impacted your body's homeostatic levels or sleep patterns. Environmental factors could be toxins, pollutants, prescribed medicines, lack of sunlight (Vitamin D deficiency), alcohol or non-prescribed drugs etc.


### The Immediate and Long Term Fixes

Please treat Anxiety as a **serious** concern. You were born perfect, no matter how you came on to this earth. You ARE perfect, and Anxiety impacts your ability to see that.

1. Remember that **meditation** can change the physical pathways of your brain (grey matter) within only a few short weeks. So why on earth would you not investigate ways to learn this simple technique?

My suggestion for new comers to meditation is not to join a class. Stay out of the larger groups where you may feel unsettled to begin. There are may sites available to us these days on the web that provide instant access to free meditation resources. One such website that I love and visit all the time is www.soundcloud.com. Simply search for the word Meditation and start with a guided meditation instead of meditation music. Artists such as David Ji or Deepak Chopra are perfect to start your search with.

20 minutes a day, 3x a week over 3 weeks will make a huge impact on your mental state.

2. Again, if you have moved straight past Stress and into Anxiety, the first thing to do is seek support; Support from friends (being honest with them), support from family (asking them to take over some of the chores), and scheduling some fun coffee dates with your most positive friends.

Do NOT spend time with friends who are prone to complaint, or gossip, as your energy will match that of the people you spend the most time with.

3. Seek out either a functional doctor or nutritionist to check your hormone levels. Anxiety and Depression are very difficult to pull out of if your brain has stopped producing the perfect match of chemicals for optimal brain function.
4. Skip to the Stress Relief section now. An extensive list of techniques is provided and equally relevant.

# Arthritis

### The Low Down

Arthritis is caused when you feel unloved, or are harboring a deep resentment towards another person.

Arthritis will manifest in areas of your body depending on other emotions also. Such as arthritic fingers relate to feeling anger or worry. Each finger relates to a different area of life (see a breakdown of these in under the heading 'fingers' further in this chapter). Again, the information provided below are the steps I myself have used or witnessed and thus know the power of their truth.

## The Fix

In order to help you, I will shed some more light on my own dalliance with Arthritis. I had been suffering only a few months, but the swelling had come on intensely and it was impacting my ability to drive and type.

Luckily my own arthritis was localised to only my index and middle fingers on both hands. When I spent 2 days alone to reflect and deal with this affliction, I honoured the pain and was determined to change my beliefs.

What I found was that I was unhappy about how I was being influenced by someone else (Anger). The moment I chose to reflect on this person with joy and love in my heart and see that their influence was out of their own fear, my frustration abated and my grasp on my own future was once again secure.

My arthritis did not disappear over night, but it did abate within 2 days with no signs of pain or swelling by day four. By no means is this an easy task to follow. I was lucky that I had 2 days alone without interruption to perform this review (The Health Hug Challenge). Many people will tell me they don't have that liberty; I say, what could be more important than your health?  2 days off work to reflect, or a lifetime of pain?

# Asthma (or breathing problems)

### The Emotional Low Down

You are feeling smothered, whether by someone, or by a situation out of your control.  Perhaps you have an over bearing partner or parent, or someone around you who makes all the decisions for you?  Perhaps you want to retire but feel you can't.

Children who show signs of asthma do well when loving routines are put in place.  Order and routine can help younger children feel they are safe and have control of the situations around them.

### The Immediate Fixes

Get rid of your plastic shower curtain.  When heated, PVC releases toxic gases that you can't see.   If you can, try to refrain from using plastic containers in the fridge or freezer.  Buy glass containers for storage only, and please refrain from using plastic bags in your Childs lunch.

Vitamin C – taking a 500mg tablet daily has been linked to a reduction in Asthmatic symptoms within weeks.

Add a small amount of magnesium to your daily routine. Magnesium has been shown to relax the muscle fibers within your lungs, making it easier to breathe.

Cut out ALL Processed foods, cows' milk, high starch and grains for a period of 4 weeks. That means no bread, no oats, no potatoes, rice, pasta, or microwave-ready foods of any kind! Your diet should consist of Vegetables, lean meats, poultry, fish, fruit, and increase your intake of Omega oils such as Olive Oil and nuts (not peanuts though). You may think this is dramatic, but I think if you're tired of struggling to breathe, wouldn't you prefer to try anything to get your quality of life back?

### The Long Term Fix

Again, reflecting on the cause, and changing your thought pattern and belief about that situation will allow your body to start healing itself

## Back Pain

### The Emotional Low Down

Where is the pain in your back? Each area of your back represents a different emotion as shown in the Emotional Self diagram at the end of chapter 7.

- Upper Back – Feeling of being unloved
- Mid Back – Guilt

- Lower Back – Financial Fear or anxiety over lack of money. (Haven't we all suffered through this one at some point in time!?)

## The Immediate Fixes

Skip to the section on Pain Relief and choose which works for you.

For Lower Back pain, simple pelvic circles (as if you are using a hula hoop), works wonders for releasing any emotional constriction. And lets be honest, it just feels good anyway. What a relief!

## The long term fixes

To lower your budget for osteopaths or chiropractic visits, sit quietly away from distraction, close your eyes, and breathe consciously through your nose. When you are feeling relaxed, focus your attention on the area of your back that is in pain and repeat out loud "Why is there pain?" I have found that if you have truly retreated into an area where you feel safe and undisturbed, and have fully relaxed, the answer will come freely. You may in fact not need to perform this exercise, as you may already know the cause based on the break down above.

Once you have the reason, spend time quietly with your eyes closed, reflecting on whether the statement is indeed true. For example:

I am stressed because I have no job and am struggling to pay my bills, meaning I have lower back pain.

Financial pressure comes when you aren't entirely certain (100%) of the exact amount of money you owe, and when each bill is owed. Spend time writing out each bill, the amount, who to, on what date is it due. Then call the businesses where bills are overdue and ask about payment options. 99% of all companies (yes, even the one man bands!) just want to be paid, and will be happy that you called. 9 times out of 10, you will be offered a 3-month respite or a payment scheme over a period of time. Make sure you write down what ever you have promised so you don't get confused over your bills!

Anytime bills come your way, don't leave the envelope unopened. Open it, and place the bill in a pile next to your computer and add the amount onto the bill ledger so your brain KNOWS it is being looked after.

If you sit quietly for long enough, you may even allow your brain to come up with other ways in which to make a bit of money! Get your kids involved in making cupcakes and sell them on the roadside one weekend. Have a garage sale to get rid of some of the clutter in your house! Offer to clean your neighbour's houses.

To summarize, it is time to work through the background to your back pain, and replace your thoughts and feelings with the opposing thoughts.

If you feel guilt, really ponder on the guilt and ask whether your guilt is warranted or self-imposed. Change the scenario in your head and see it from someone else's point of view. Work it from every angle until you reach a point where you forgive yourself. What is in the past is DONE.

If you feel unloved, there are other ways to reclaim that love. You only feel unloved if you don't first love yourself. If you loved yourself full heartedly, you wouldn't have the need to have other people loving you to make you feel good. Please reflect on what makes you amazing. Because you truly are! Join some social organisations, meet new people, or buy a pet! Whatever works for you. But know that because you are part of my family (in that your energy is linked with mine) you are definitely loved. And I thank you for being so perfect in my eyes.

# Brain

## The Emotional Low Down

Adults who suffer brain tumors are often times those people who also have taken on too many hats, or a large project, or something in life that has become overwhelming to them.

The Brain is linked with the emotion of "Overwhelm".

This summary of course does not consider brain INJURY or birth defects. However it is my strong belief and experience that most brain function anomalies can be reversed through changing the brain's neuroplasticity and through proper nutrition.

I myself was healed from Petit Mal Epilepsy when I was only 7 years old by my fathers' total disregard of the medical diagnosis. He hated standing by as he watched his daughter being plugged up to machines day in and day out, whilst losing memory and personality traits along the way. So he went half way across the world to find a cure. Within a few months of simply taking a third of a teaspoon of Epsom Salts (Pure Magnesium salts) in a glass of water daily, my brain healed itself and my need for drugs disappeared over night to the bewilderment of the doctors who were treating me.

Know this; your brain needs a certain level of minerals to remain in optimal health. Many children these days are depleted of these natural minerals due to the foods they eat (think; lots of sugar and carbs, and the mineral deficient soils within which we grow our food), hence the increased onset of A.D.H.D and other behavioural issues that were basically non existent before 1950.

## The Immediate Fixes

Ask your Chemist for L-Glutamine, (an essential neurotransmitter in the brain) to boost production in order to help with memory, focus and concentration. (If you can't get to a chemist, then Glutamic acid is naturally found in foods such as Bone Broth, Cottage Cheese, Spirulina, and Asparagus.

Slow your thoughts down. Start writing lists. Create order in your home. Reduce the amount of chaos.

Consciously BREATHE (In through the nose please, to gain instant access to your brain, and deep breaths; none of this shallow breathing!)

Reframe all of your thoughts. You MUST reduce the overwhelm. So here's an example: if you know that all hell breaks loose the moment your kids get home from school – get ready for them! Plan NOT to work between 3-6pm, fully dedicating yourself to those kids instead of trying to multi task. Plan in advance their arrival by creating a game that will keep them busy for 20 mins. In short, change how you SEE the situation. It is your perception of the situation that is causing the over load.

And please seek out and inject more FUN and JOY in your life.

### The long term fixes

Replenish the minerals in your diet. Eat for health and nutrition. The more anti-oxidants you can get in your diet the better also. See a nutritionist or research your needs online.

Increase your intake of Magnesium, Zinc and Omega 3's.

# Breast / Chest

### The Emotional Low Down

The breast and chest area is connected with lack of self. When was the last time you put yourself first? Almost all of the ladies I was in the Chemo ward with, and hundreds of others I have spoken to since, have all agreed that they are "givers" first and foremost. The husband and children come first; once all the chores are done, and you've given your personal time to volunteer at the local school fair, your own needs seem to become a distant memory.

How many times have you sat around a coffee table with friends agreeing how wonderful it would be to have an hour off just so you can sit and breathe!? If this is you, then watch out; these are the people most prone to recurring chest infections and breast cancer.

### The Fix

Spend time reflecting on how you can reclaim your sense of self. If you always put others first, you are not truly living this life on your terms. Surely there is room in this life for everyone? Even you. Start by adding an activity that you enjoy, that is considered decadent to you, just once a week. Then, plan to take 15 minutes each day, where you are able to read your favourite book, or take a short walk. Plan a vacation with your friends. Whatever it takes to find the old YOU again!

# Bowel Problems (IBS) / Blood in stool

### The Emotional Low Down

The bowel and abdomen are intrinsically linked to the emotion of overwhelming fear

### The Immediate Fixes

Blood in stool:

Is the blood in your stool dark (old) or bright (new)? What this can tell your doctor is whether your blood has travelled from your intestine or stomach (dark) or whether it is localized in your rectum (bright)

If the stool is dark red, it may pay to help your body rebuild its mucous lining in the gut and intestines. 2 very easy options are available for you:

Probiotics and Glutamine

Probiotics:

During Chemo, or after a course of Antibiotics, the microorganisms lining your gut that aid in digestion and nutrient absorption are killed off. Your body needs help to increase the count of those microorganisms again. Adding a cup of Probiotic yoghurt to your daily breakfast will aid in that replacement. An adequate count of Probiotics in your gut is also linked to a reduction in Lactose Intolerance, and reduced symptoms from allergies! There are some very good probiotic supplements on the market today if you aren't a fan of yoghurt. Find ones with the highest probiotic count possible (40-70 Billion CFU+).

Glutamine:

Glutamine (or L-Glutamine) is an amino acid that improves the mucous membrane lining of the digestive tract, amongst other things, aiding in the efficiency of your entire digestive system. A study published in the medical journal Lancet, examined 20 hospitised patients and found that supplementing with L-glutamine decreased intestinal permeability significantly. You can ask at your local health food store or chemist for this product - best supplemented with Vitamin B12 to avoid excessive buildup.

**The long term fixes**

Ask yourself what you are most fearful of. What can you do to face that fear and accept it or reduce its impact on your thoughts? Read the section on Abdominal Pain for more.

# Cancer

## The Emotional Low Down

Well, this is the big one. Cancer is on the increase, and the plight to find a cure is now a $3Billion industry. Cancer is caused by a deep hurt or resentment. As with the Texan research, recognize what happened between 18-24 months prior to diagnosis, where you gave yourself permission to pull the "kill switch". Whether it was statements like "I can't live like this any more!" or a divorce, death of a loved one, a job loss, or anger at another person. Add to that the area where the Cancer forms and you'll understand how to stop cancer from returning!

For instance, Breast Cancer is allowed to form by the victim "putting others first" all the time, effectively lacking any love for yourself. Breast Cancer patients are usually the matriarchs of the family, the givers, the supporters, the big lovers at the detriment of their own health. If you reclaim your own joy, forgiveness, love and zest for life again, there is no room in your breast for the return of any Cancer ever again!

## The Immediate fixes

OK, so the obvious fix is to do whatever your Oncologist tells you! In the mean time know that Cancer feeds on Sugar, so eradicate all forms of sugar (including simple carbs) from your diet.

## The Long term fix

Love thy body. Love thy self. The less stress and judgment in your life, the better! The healing program is outlined in earlier in this book. I suggest giving this a try. What have you got to loose!

In short, make the following life long changes:

Diet + joy + peace of mind + eradication of external stressors = lifelong health. And believe me, you don't have to move to Tibet to find such an existence ☺.

# Constipation

### The Emotional Low Down

Stress or Anxiety will be a prevalent factor, so immediately reflect on all the possible stressors in your life and work to dissipate their impact immediately.

### The Immediate Fixes

Increase the amounts of fluids you drink to loosen your bowel movements.

Eat High fibre foods such as;

Raw vegetables, beans, fruit, high fibre cereals, bananas

Increase your activity levels - even going for a slow gentle walk will help.

Milk of Magnesia. Milk of Magnesia helps to assist in bowel movements by retaining water in your stool, making the stool feel bulkier and more persistent in wanting to move

Metamucil (found in any chemist) - assists in the same way, but by adding bulk through additional fibre.

**The long term fixes**

Find out what is causing you stress at this particular moment, and deal with it head on. Read the chapter on Stress earlier in this book.

# Colds

### The Low Down

A Cold is a virus that has been allowed into your body due to an under performing immune system. This can be precluded by bouts of stress or environmental causes, which break down the protective mucous layer in your nasal and throat passages. Know this, if your protective membranes are in optimal health, there is no such cold that can break through - you're naturally a tough cookie.

### The Immediate Fixes

Echinacea (rawest form if you can), garlic, and colloidal silver.

Increase your Antioxidant intake, and fluid consumption to support the extraction process of any waste products. Keep frozen berries in the freezer, and add these to smoothies, or thaw and add to yoghurt or your morning muesli as a great kick-starter to the day.

Check your PH levels. Buy a saliva PH testing kit from your local Health Food store. Optimal PH levels should be between 7 and 7.5. Anything above or below that means your cells are struggling to perform. Repair quickly by eradicating any acid forming foods from your diet (Coffee, red meat, sugar and starch for instance).

And of course increase your intake of laughter! The more you laugh, the faster you'll heal. This is especially true with children. The more you get them to dance like silly aliens, the less time they'll spend off sick! Tickle Monsters is just what the doctor ordered.

**The long term fixes**

Adhering to a healthy diet where your ingestion of alkaline forming foods is in greater proportion to your acid forming foods and beverages, and supporting natural production of all minerals and vitamins in your body by increasing raw and organic foods is a great place to start.

Drinking more water (with lemon to reduce the acidity of the water), will assist your liver, kidneys and bowel to eradicate waste as fast as possible.

(See Nose for further quick fixes)

# Coughs

**The Emotional Low Down**

As with the Throat, coughing is a symptom of being unable to express yourself. Perhaps you're not being heard at work, or you're afraid to mention something to your partner or friend? Note, this is for dry coughs that seem recurring or persistent that you just can't seem to shake through modern medicine. A cough caused by mucous from a cold is different, and is covered below.

### The Immediate Fixes

Colloidal silver kills everything (my personal belief although there is mixed debate on this subject, so please do your research and make up your own mind). I keep a bottle handy in my kitchen (and a few drops in the ear works wonders for kids with ear infections too!), as well as a bottle of Coconut Water (see the benefits outlined in chapter 9.

### The long term fixes

What is it that you want to say but can't? Understand why, and who you need to talk to and resolve this issue head on. If you can't speak your truth then find another way, perhaps even by writing a letter, or journaling your thoughts.

## Diarrhea

### The Emotional Low Down

This is typically another GUT problem caused by fear or rejection. Often manifests in children when they are frightened of mummy leaving them behind, or not being loved due to possibly feeling that they have 'upset' mummy/daddy.  Children who are sensitive can often pick up stress from their parents (work stress that comes home with you) or teachers.  Obviously Diarrhea can be caused by eating foods that disagree with you, but if there seems to be no cause, stop and think about a possible emotional link instead.

**The Immediate Fixes**

Whilst suffering from Diarrhea, avoid foods that make it worse, such as; Dairy products, fried foods, caffeine, chocolate

**DO eat bland foods** which are easily digested, such as;

Bananas, rice, toast, crackers and broth

**Stay hydrated** by drinking small amounts throughout the day.  Large amounts at once can cause you to be sick, hence take lots of little sips.

**Do NOT** drink very chilled fluids as this irritates your intestines.  Try drinking room temperature fluids in small amounts.

Dehydration can manifest through symptoms of **dizziness, or weakness** - if these symptoms occur please see a doctor immediately.  **Potassium** is the first mineral that is depleted through severe diarrhea. (Hence Bananas are a great food to increase intake during this time)

Ask your Chemist for **L-Glutamine,** which helps by balancing mucous production in the gut.

### The long term fixes

As with all other ailments, retreat into a safe quiet space, and reflect on what it is that you are most fearful of. Once you have the answer (technique outlined in Section 3 of this book), you can then begin to address the cause.

Add Probiotics to your daily routine (yoghurts or supplements). Probiotics are live microorganisms similar to those found in our own gut and assist in reforming the healthy lining of your gut. (Also helps eliminate allergies, gas and bloating)

## Ear aches

### The Emotional Low Down

What is it that you don't want to hear? What is it that you are blocking out? See the Long Term Fixes for more information.

### The Immediate Fixes

Believe it or not, Pure Proof Vodka or Gin works a treat! Who would have thought! Pure alcohol kills any bugs in your outer ear, and can clear out any blockages. However, if your hearing is going you will need to work through the emotional cause as outlined below. Please refrain from poking anything in to your ear, or your child's as it is an inner organ that is extremely fragile and easily damaged through touch.

**The long term fixes**

Spend time reflecting on what message in life you refuse to hear or listen to. Are you sick and tired of people telling you what to do? Are you fed up with your family telling you to do something (such as retire)? Or are you just plain tired with all the excess noise in life, therefore craving a quieter existence? If the latter, instead of going deaf for the cause why not move to a quieter environment where there is less noise? Or stand up and speak out against any pressure from other people.

Earaches in children are often found when a stubborn child (weren't we all?) disagrees with being told what to do, or how they were told off by their parents. How do you fix this with a child who won't listen? Find a middle ground by talking through impacts and consequences with your child when they're in a 'good' mood. Get THEM to decide the right punishment and make sure you draw or write this oath on a piece of paper together, that they can refer to in the event of that punishment being undertaken. If your child feels they have some say in the manner, (in other words, they feel heard) earaches invariable go away.

Whatever the cause of your own ear pain, you should determine to take the time now to change the message so it's either diluted or no longer forthcoming.

# Eyes – Vision or Conjunctivitis

**The Emotional Low Down**

What don't you want to address?  What in your life do you not like the look of?  Is there anything in your future that you are not looking forward to?

## The Fix

As mentioned in Section One, I healed my own eyes from Presbyopia loss of the elasticity of the lens of the eye due to aging) within 24 hours.  Reflect on what is causing you concern (The Healing process is outlined in detail in Section 3 of this book) and then address it.  I chose to reframe how I thought about the situation.  I was frustrated that I was working in a role that was not where I was longing to be.  It was at odds with my values and my passion.  I was on the cusp of breaking into a new career but was unable to make the immediate leap.


To resolve this issue, I accepted my predicament and chose to look at it from another angle, a 'reframe', if you will, in order to accept the situation and be at peace with it.  Each day I spent in that role, was another opportunity to help a coworker.  Each day meant I was guaranteed an income to assist with my career move.  Each day meant I had the opportunity to be social and make new friends.  I reframed my thinking, and addressed my frustration by first acknowledging the cause.  I then meditated on feeling excited about my first day back at work.  I chose to see my working arrangement as a gift from God, somewhere I was supposed to be in order to help others.

Name your feelings to expose them.

# Fingers

## The Emotional Low Down

Each finger has a different emotional attachment.

- Thumbs – Intellect and worry
- Index Finger – Ego and Fear
- Ring Finger – Partnership and Grief
- Middle Finger – Anger and Sexuality
- Little Finger – Family pretense

## The Immediate Fixes

Tingling:

May be caused by peripheral neuropathy, so check with your chemist or natural health store for supplemental Glutamine to aid the restoration of the neural sheeths

Arthritic:

Read the chapter on Pain Relief, and increase your intake of Capsicum, salmon and Turmeric, which have all been linked to reducing arthritic pain nicely within a few weeks.

## The long term fixes

Skip now to the DIY Bible. Reflect on what it is that has caused this pain, and deal to it immediately. You would benefit nicely from the steps in the DIY Health Hug.

# Face

## The Emotional Low Down

Anything relating to the face (acne, scars, scabs, rashes etc) represents our ego and who we show to the world. This is a difficult one for most of us to get our head around, as naturally we all like to think we have no ego. But having an ego is a good thing, it defines who we are and why we are different from the next person.

## The Fix

Come to love yourself for who you are. Get over your ego and public face. This is not what defines you. As you become less aware of how others perceive you and that you hold the power to create happiness in your life, you will learn to let go of your image. You are not defined by your dress size. You are not defined by your beauty. You are defined by your soul. Reflect and understand this to believe in yourself wholeheartedly, and all facial issues will disappear. I highly recommend looking in to the works and books by Louise L. Hay, Byron Katie, and Brandon Bays.

# Feet

## The Emotional Low Down

Interestingly, feet have been linked with our deepest understanding of ourselves. Who we are, where we are in life and how we fit in.

## The Fix

If you have tingling, numbness or arthritis, read those sub heading also.

If you have pain, read the Pain Relief Chapter

However, for deeper issues, please review the DIY Health Hug

## Hearing – See ears

## Headaches and Migraines

### The Emotional Low Down

Stop being self-critical.  And stop over-thinking things! You may be putting a lot of pressure on yourself that other people don't actually expect.

### The Immediate Fixes

Laughter releases endorphins in your brain, and reduces pain instantly.

Rub from the base of your thumb to the tip of the thumb to activate your reflexology points for your brain and head.  Doing this vigorously for a few minutes helps every time.

Or simply rub your ear lobes where many of the same activation points are found.  Otherwise jump to the appendices to find the exact reflexology points on the hands and feet.

### The long term fixes

Why are you being so hard on yourself?  You are perfect.  If you suffer from repetitive headaches, I would ask that you see a medical doctor to ensure there is nothing more sinister going on.

Add magnesium and selenium to your diet.

Reduce arterial constrictive agents such as caffeine and nicotine.

Go to the DIY Health Hug section - Headaches are also a great excuse to schedule in a few "pamper-me" days to have something to look forward to.


# Hot flushes

### The Low Down

Caused by your brains thermostat (the hypothalamus) getting a little confused.  If you're nearing the onset of menopause, hot flushes can be due to low levels of estrogen.  If not, then Stress is a well-known activator also.


### The Immediate Fixes

Many Hormone Replacement Therapy drugs, and often Radiation Therapy, can send messages to your brain to activate menopausal symptoms.  One of those is Hot Flushes.  These hot flushes are predominantly worse in women whose liver or adrenal function is less than optimal.  (So hint ladies: do everything you can to get your adrenals and liver back in homeostasis to reduce these symptoms for good)

Black Cohosh or Sage:  Fabulous if your liver is working well also.  These herbs help stimulate estrogen production

Cinnamon or Turmeric:  Both cooling agents.  Add cinnamon to your morning coffee, add turmeric to dinners, or sprinkle over grilled fish.


If all else fails, I've found that if you wake in the middle of the night with a temperature that is raging, immediately capture what thought it was that you were thinking before you woke.   9 times out of 10, you will find that the thought was one that does not serve you.  You might be reflecting on a stressful conversation that you had that day and your brain goes in to hyper-drive.  Or you may be worrying about what to do with the kids tomorrow.  Or a memory from your past was lingering and causing you angst.


None of these are relaxing, releasing thoughts.  When you're mind feels a spike in stress and your hormones are already up the "whack", the FASTEST way to stop the heat is to instantly change your thoughts.  Have a happy thought on hand.  Tap in to it each night when you wake.  Swapping out these thoughts will save you hours of tossing and turning, and will be my simple gift to you.  It really works.


**The long term fixes**

Balanced Hormone regulation is your number one priority, along with ongoing stress management practices.

# Kidney

### The Emotional Low Down

As with the Adrenals, this is our center for held Anxiety and an uncertainty on how to care for ourselves.

### The Fix

To support the transport of toxins and dead cells from your system, aid your kidneys by drinking clean, alkaline fluids.

If your liver is underperforming, your kidneys take the brunt and overflow of the toxins, which then build up and impact your kidneys too. You must assist both organs at the same time so as not to overload one or the other during times of stress. One cannot perform well without the full support of the other. See options for the Liver below.

# Liver

### The Emotional Low Down

Our central store for our Anger

### The Immediate Fixes

Be careful if you choose to detoxify your liver only. Your liver usually becomes toxic due to an imbalance elsewhere also. If you suddenly change the toxicity of your liver, all that waste will be shifted to your kidneys for removal. Are your kidneys up for that? If you can, opt for a total body cleanse. Or detoxify slowly by eradicating all acidic foods from your diet and increasing the alkaline intake.

To assist the flow of toxins through your liver, drink more clean fluids.

## Memory

### The Low Down

Unless there is a direct correlation between medications you are on and your memory loss (as advised by your medical care giver), the onset of memory loss, or short-term recall problems is usually a treatable affliction if caught quickly. If honest, the memory loss is more a "Brain Fuzz" rather than an inability to recall memory. If you so choose to recall something of importance, you will. However you may move about your day forgetting to do things, and forgetting someone's name within 3 seconds of meeting them.

### The Immediate Fixes

To remove the Fuzz over your mind, add more Omega-3 rich foods to your diet to promote a more seamless neural flow (Salmon, Walnuts, wild rice, edamame (soy bean)

Investigate options for learning meditation. Remember the research outlined earlier in this book talking about how 20 mins (3x weekly) meditation changes the neuroplasticity (neural pathways) in the brain? It is never too late to learn to meditate. To help, you may like to go to website www.soundcloud.com and search for "Guided Meditation". That way, you can learn and practice in the comfort of your own home.

**The long term fixes**

Diet and toxicity have been linked to the onset of ailments such as Alzheimer's (as well as most other brain related diseases). A recent study done by Rush University Medical Center in Chicago showed that diet alone helped reduce the symptoms of Alzheimer's by as much as 53%. Patients were told to eat a diet full of the following:

- Green Leafy Vegetables (predominantly for the intake of Vitamins C and A)
- Almonds/Cashews/Brazil Nuts
- Berries
- Beans (high in Fiber and Protein)
- White meats, Fish/Chicken

Also, this is probably one of the only times I'm going to tell you to INCREASE your caffeine intake! Recent studies done in Sweden and Denmark has shown that moderate intake of caffeine can reduce the onset of Dementia and Alzheimer's by up to 65%.

For any such symptoms, please see a health professional.

Increase your count of social interactions. Research has shown that having a fun, social network has a strong influence on reducing the onset of memory loss, and increases longevity.


# Mouth (Sores, Inflammation)

### The Low Down

Closed mindedness. Perhaps you are not open to new ideas and need to befriend these ideas as possibilities.

**The Immediate Fixes**

**- Dry Mouth:**

There are many great natural techniques that you can use to aid in the production of saliva. Obviously the first choice is to **drink more alkaline fluids**; however some people are limited to the amount of fluids they can ingest due to direction from their medical team.

One of the BEST remedies is to place a small (about 2 drops only) amount of pure **ECHINACEA** on the tip of your tongue. Yes, you will find your tongue may go temporarily numb, but the saliva production is instant, therefore worth it. You can pick up a "Tincture" of pure Echinacea if you ask nicely from most Health Stores.

If you're travelling, or away from such an option; make yourself some yummy **Ice chips or cubes**. **Tart** flavours are best; such as Lemon, Lime, or Grapefruit. If you prefer something sweeter, add some Manuka Honey (UMH10+) to Hot Lemon water prior to placing in the freezer.

**- Mouth Ulcers:**

Avoid Spicy or hot foods!

Lower your intake of acid forming foods (such as red meat, sugar, diary, pasta and white flour). Try to up your intake in Alkaline foods to bring your system back into balance (Rule of thumb, anything green is Alkaline. Lemons are amazingly alkaline too but will sting ulcers)

Make a dilute solution of baking soda and warm water as a rinse (although personally this tastes horrid, and doesn't go well if you are also suffering through Nausea!) This does however promote the lowering of acidity in your mouth.

Spreading egg yolk across your ulcers will form a barrier and lessen the pain.

Try Glutamine (5grams) mixed with about 3/4 cup of water. Rinse, gargle and hold it in your mouth for about 30 seconds, then swallow. Do this 3x daily to speed up healing of your mouth/throat.

Avoid all over the counter or grocery sold Mouth Wash/rinses as they include Alcohol, which promotes further opening of your wounds.

**The long term fixes**

Reflect on what ideas you are currently rejecting. Even if you don't believe in those ideas, if you could find it in your heart to understand why the other person believes in them so much, you accept that there is always another option, other than your own. Accept that there are other beliefs and ideas that are just as good as your own. Acknowledgement is the perfect start for all healing.

# Nausea

### The Emotional Low Down

Stress or anxiety.  Also linked with the sense of dread

### The Immediate Fixes

There are many drugs on the market these days that affectively get rid of symptoms of Nausea either by preventing it, or reducing it.

If you are not currently taking Anti-Nausea medication, and want to try natural remedies, here are a few hints and tricks;

- Eating and drinking in small amounts, on a regular basis helps to underwhelm your senses, hence avoiding the onset of nausea.
- Eat dry foods such as crackers or toast
- Peppermint or Ginger Tea helps reduce Nausea
- Change your diet momentarily so as to avoid foods with intense odours (avoid restaurants, food halls, and foods cooked with spices and aromatics)

### The long term fixes

Consult the chapter in this book on Stress Relief to reduce the impact that stress has over your health.

# Neck

### The Emotional Low Down

Inflexibility. Are you holding on to an outcome and rejecting another point of view or possibility?

### The Fix

As in the DIY Health Hug, deal with the cause and your pain should abate.

A good reflexology point to rub is at the base of your big toe (in the bend).

I am also a firm believer in Chiropractic or Osteopathy to realign your spine and spinal nerves to enhance neural function.

# Nose (Stuffy, runny, sinuses)

### The Emotional Low Down

You have a need for recognition which you are not getting.

Often a child may show signs of a long-term runny or stuffy nose, yet the parent is adamant they are showing that child a lot of love and showering them with cuddles. All children are different; many of which have a strong desire for praise and positive feedback constantly. This is your ideal cure for the child with the never ending runny nose, not the usual cuddles that work on other children.

### The Immediate Fixes

If viral, see the fixes in the Colds section

To clear up a stuffy nose (possibly to aid a child to sleep) simply press **firmly** on the sinus tunnel on both sides of your nose for 1-2 minutes. Then swipe firmly away towards your ears. Also press on the sinus points just between the eyes on the outer bridge of the nose. Once you have done this, sit up for 1 minute to allow the sinus to run freely.

### The long term fixes

What is the cause of the nose problem? Where are you looking for your recognition? Is there a way to get that recognition elsewhere? Or can you say something in order to provoke it? Perhaps you could reframe your thinking, so you remove the need for this adulation?

If your child has a problem, try to ask probing questions, and give them lots of praise and cuddles.


## Numbness or Tingling:

### The Immediate Fixes

This is often caused by peripheral neuropathy if not a skin irritation.

**Glutamine** has been shown to reduce these symptoms nicely. Ask your local chemist or Oncologist for Glutamine tablets or powder.


Increasing movement (fluid motions) and stretching will reinvigorate your body's natural neural pathway function also.   Our circulation can become "sticky" when we stagnate.

# PMS / Period Pain

## The Low Down

Many teens go on the contraceptive pill to stop period pain as it stops that pathway of neural activity between the brain and the ovaries, very similar to opiate drugs.  If you stop this message early in your development however, your brain never learns how to connect, meaning all hell breaks loose as you age and eventually come off the pill.

To get scientific on you; your pituitary gland (brain) will not send the right messages to stimulate hormonal balance in your body.  You'll either become Estrogen Dominant, or Progesterone Depleted.


Period Pain is the body's way of telling you that there is an imbalance in the first place.  Hence, clients should be told how to stimulate hormonal regulation naturally.


## The Immediate Fixes

There are some easy things you should IMMEDIATELY do (don't wait until next month).

1.  DIY Reflexology on your hand - press firmly for 5 mins EVERY night (whilst watching TV etc).  This activates neural activity to your Adrenals. (Picture is in the appendix – Look for the Adrenals point specifically)

2. Reduce your intake of any Caffeine and Alcohol for 2 months. Both spark up stress on your liver and Adrenals and limit hormone production.
3. Reduce dairy. If you can, go without for 4 weeks
4. It helps to do a liver detox to rule out Liver Congestion from the equation also (but this is a secondary option).
5. Remember when you have heavy periods, it's VERY important to **replace your Magnesium** (Epsom Salts from your local chemist $8 is an easy option - add to bath or tiny amount to your drinking water daily).
6. Period <u>pain</u> is caused by an increase in Pro-inflammatory chemicals in your system. To decrease the pain (not the cause) you should **increase your intake** of counter-inflammatory FOODS: Essential fats (Avocados, Olive Oil), fish oil (or fish) or Flaxseed (LSA is easy to sprinkle on your cereal each morning).
7. And **AVOID** Inflammatory foods: Margarine, Vegetable or Corn Oils

Sounds like a lot to do, but once you've got into a routine, it becomes easier. If you're having pain now, once you reach Menopause, you'll have one hell of a time. So best work on this NOW!

For teenagers, instead of reaching the Pill to help with pain, why not help them balance optimal hormonal production by looking at their diet. Get them off those high sugar drinks and on to green smoothies as the first priority.

# Rash / Skin

## The Emotional Low Down

Frustration

## The Immediate Fixes

Coconut water and Coconut oil have been linked with regeneration of skin cells, and is easy to apply after your daily shower. Choose the Coconut water option if you don't like the smell.

See also the point on your pinky finger (smallest) in the reflexology chart in the appendix for Skin.

# Stomach

## The Emotional Low Down

Dread / Fear

## The Fixes

(Also see Nausea)

Add Probiotics to your daily diet (whether in yoghurt form or through supplements) to aid in Villi stimulation and regeneration on your gut lining.

See also the point in the centre of your palm for stomach and intestinal reflexology points on the chart in the appendix.

(Also see Acid Reflux)

## Taste (as with mouth)

### The Low Down

Closed mindedness.  You are not open to new ideas and need to befriend these ideas as possibilities.

### The Immediate Fixes

Some medications may cause a momentary loss of taste.  99% of the time, this sense will come back after a few short weeks after completion of any treatment.  If it does not however, ask your doctor for a prescription of ZINC supplement, which helps your body to regain taste.

Spark your taste senses during this time, by adding TART or Sweet foods to your diet.

## Throat

### The Emotional Low Down

As with Coughing, the throat is linked with an inability to express yourself.  You have something to say but aren't able to say it.

### The Fix

(See also Cough, and Mouth)

Additional Short Overviews:

# Heart

### The Emotional Low Down

Depending on the affliction, the heart, being our "heart centre", the centre of our soul, is linked to emotion and joy. Think deep long standing emotional issues, or lack of joy in ones life

# Hips

### The Emotional Low Down

Fear of moving forward, not having anything to look forward to, therefore holding on to the now

# Knees

### The Emotional Low Down

Stubborn Pride and Ego. Has it been knocked lately?

Know any men with knee problems needing surgery? Reflexology and acupuncture will help in the short term. Helping someone to gain back his or her pride will allow the knee to heal itself.

# Legs

### The Emotional Low Down

Fear of the future. Fear of moving forward

# The Health Hug's Key Message

Find the joy in every moment and in every one.  Become more of a witness instead of being involved.  It will amaze you what miracles you start to see about your average daily life.

And know this; you are loved.

And you are FRIGGIN' AMAZING!!!

# Appendix

## Easy Reflexology Points for the foot

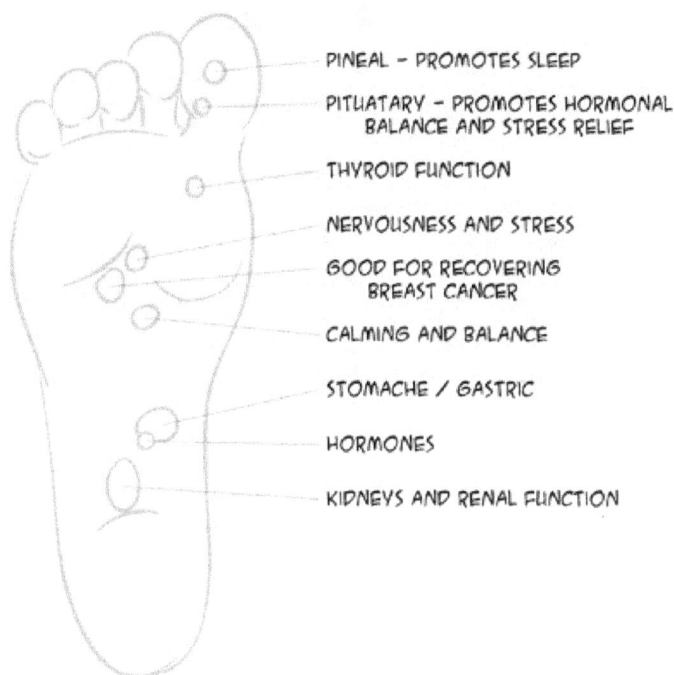

PINEAL – PROMOTES SLEEP

PITUATARY – PROMOTES HORMONAL
    BALANCE AND STRESS RELIEF

THYROID FUNCTION

NERVOUSNESS AND STRESS

GOOD FOR RECOVERING
    BREAST CANCER

CALMING AND BALANCE

STOMACHE / GASTRIC

HORMONES

KIDNEYS AND RENAL FUNCTION

# Reflexology Points for the Hand

## Ta

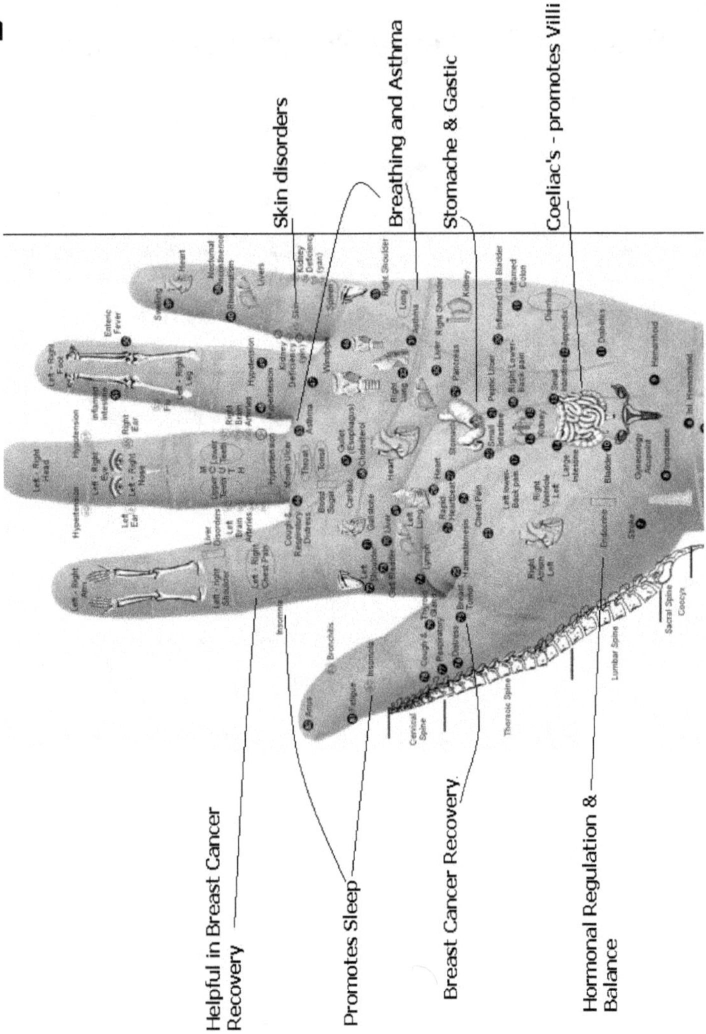

Skin disorders
Breathing and Asthma
Stomache & Gastic
Coeliac's - promotes Villi
Helpful in Breast Cancer Recovery
Promotes Sleep
Breast Cancer Recovery.
Hormonal Regulation & Balance

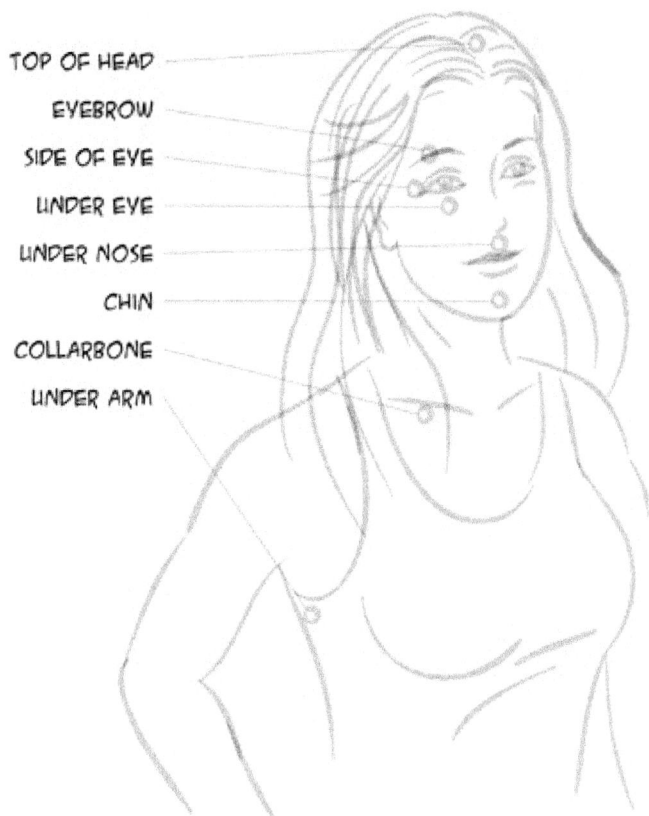

TOP OF HEAD
EYEBROW
SIDE OF EYE
UNDER EYE
UNDER NOSE
CHIN
COLLARBONE
UNDER ARM

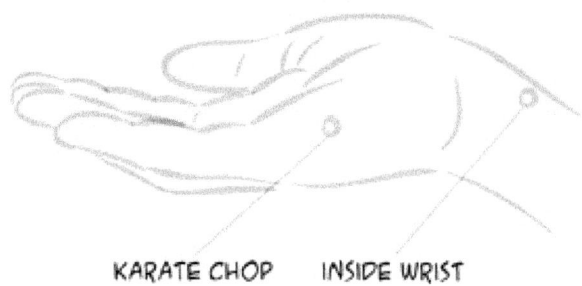

KARATE CHOP     INSIDE WRIST

# ABOUT THE AUTHOR

Ani Wilson is a philanthropist with a huge heart. She founded The Health Hug in 2013 in order to supply a website that offered free resources for anyone in need after finding a gap in the availability of instant help when she was diagnosed with Cancer in 2010. She often runs free seminars about the impact of stress on health, and many of her current coaching clients are pro-bono due to her deep need to help others.

Ani has lived and breathed upper management corporate for over 20 years, and always prided herself on her ability to handle extreme levels of stress well. What was once a habitual state of being, is now her passionate cause.

Her message?

"Stress is NOT a requirement in life. Stress is unnecessary and easily avoided if you know how. It bugs me that so much money and time is wasted when people realise this fact. My mission is to save people money and make sure they find themselves in that happy state quickly!"

www.ingramcontent.com/pod-product-compliance
Lightning Source LLC
LaVergne TN
LVHW052020080426
835513LV00018B/2100